Contents

Foreword

What is a hurdle? By definition a "hurdle is a barrier which contestants must leap over, placed at certain intervals around a track to complete a race." A "hurdle" can also be described as "a difficult problem to overcome; an obstacle". On the one hand hurdles are not fun, because it means we have to overcome obstacles to complete a race which would have otherwise been somewhat straight forward without the hurdles in place. On the contrary, hurdles ensure that base level standards and competence are achieved before one can claim rights to authority, status, rights, privileges, credentials, credibility or the like. Consequently, it takes mental gumption, inner strength, determination, resilience and more to overcome hurdles; and as a direct result, we become much stronger people, for having the mental gumption, inner strength, determination, resilience and more to overcome the hurdles; the difficult problems and the obstacles in our path, before we finally reach our desired outcomes.

Human cloning and REM driven cloning is a reality and a fact of life. However, with the current hurdles in place, for which there are many hurdles; the hurdles prevent many people from reaching the desired outcome and realising simple truths which become GLARINGLY obvious once people decide to make the mental efforts to overcome their personal biases and blast through each level of "cognitive dissonance" and overcome each hurdle presented, until people reach the desired outcome to realise CONCLUSIVELY that human cloning and REM driven cloning is indeed a reality and a fact of life which **MUST** be stopped! It is my **earnest plea** that reader gives this document, as well as, ALL Mr. Donald Marshall's disclosures the **WEIGHT** of importance they deserve. Blast through your cognitive dissonances, overcome your hurdles, and once you do, you will see the simple truth, laid out right in front of your very eyes, and right in front of your very nose which has been prevalent for many decades. Life references Mr. Donald Marshall's disclosures, and Mr. Donald Marshall's eyewitness testimonies references life. Such a feat only happens when a person tells the truth. Furthermore, the lies and deceptions are so BIG and so GRAND that the simple truth appears "crazy" on the surface, because the simple truth goes counter-clockwise to the many lies and deceptions which are orchestrated on a grand scale daily. However, the truth is the truth, and the truth MUST be known. Read, print, download and share this imperative information; it is imperative information which many, many human lives depend on.

Furthermore, REM driven cloning is the **main** topic which TRULY exposes humanity's enemy: the Illuminati. Therefore, the smart and logical path to take is the path which will lead to the downfall of our enemy; and that path is to learn and fully understand the subject matter of "The Illuminati's REM driven cloning subculture". Leave nothing to chance or speculation; make sure you reach a point where you KNOW the truths discussed in this document IS a reality and a fact of life; and once you reach that stage, share Mr. Donald Marshall's documents like wildfire. Humanity's fate depends on you.

Introduction

This short document highlights Frequently Asked Questions Mr. Donald Marshall has received from the public since he first sent his letter to the world on 2nd December 2011 regarding the extent and prevalence of human cloning. This document allows the reader to have a further source of reference regarding the most pertinent information concerning the Illuminati. Readers should refer to "Empowerment by Virtue of Golden Truth" (Marshall 2015b) for a full discussion on the subject of "REM driven cloning". The main topic of discussion in this document is: "The Illuminati's REM driven cloning subculture" for which REM driven cloning is the technology and method by which Illuminati members meet in complete secrecy to discuss worldly affairs and commit crimes against humanity.

Fundamentally, the answers to the questions presented here by Mr. Donald Marshall are firsthand, eyewitness accounts through highly advanced scientific technology by the process of consciousness transfer from Mr. Marshall's original body to his REM driven clone where Mr. Donald Marshall experiences the SAME earth, only this time in a REM driven clone body, with a clarity of awareness as REM driven clone version of himself; such as how people experience the world with a clarity awareness when their consciousness resides in their original body. Consequently, Mr. Donald Marshall has met many of the world's high profile figures which Mr. Marshall has speaks of, but only as REM driven clone versions of themselves.

It is evident to the fact that Mr. Donald Marshall has met many of the high profile figures he speaks of as "REM driven clone versions" because Mr. Donald Marshall has spoken very negatively of many high profile figures in society and not ONE person in over four years has addressed Mr. Donald Marshall for the slander of her / his name. It is a serious and reputation damaging accusation to call another person a "paedophile", yet not a SINGLE high profile figure has addressed Mr. Donald Marshall on this issue or taken Mr. Donald Marshall to court to clear their name of such an accusation. Furthermore, it is illegal to cite hatred or spread hoaxes by use of a computer which would incite a public panic and cause dissension, and the punishment for citing hatred and spreading hoaxes via computer is either a fine or prison; yet Mr. Donald Marshall has not received a fine or imprisonment for his testimonies. Consequently, one should first look to the law, in order to understand that Mr. Donald Marshall IS providing accurate and detailed factual information, otherwise Mr. Donald Marshall would have been fined or imprisoned many years ago for either: slandering names, (possibly) inciting a public panic and using a computer to do so. Mr. Donald Marshall tells the truth regarding his accounts of Illuminati's REM driven cloning subculture. Consequently, it is imperative and of MONUMENTAL importance that humanity learns and understands the true nature its enemy: the Illuminati, and the Illuminati's REM driven cloning subculture, because it IS "REM driven cloning" which truly exposes the Illuminati. Read / Print / Download / Share.

List of Abbreviations:

3SG1: = Third person singular (first respondent, etc.)
DM: = Donald Marshall

Clones

Coping in real life from exposure to REM driven cloning

3SG1: How do these people cope in real life once they have been exposed to it [REM driven cloning]?

DM: How some people cope in real life is through drinking alcohol; and some people cope by taking drugs... after being exposed _to REM driven cloning_. <u>**July 2, 2012 at 11:42am**</u>

How REM driven clones are activated

3SG1: Can the Illuminati only activate your _REM driven_ clone when you are asleep?

DM: Yes. I mentioned this in the letter (Donald Marshall Proboards 2012; Marshall 2015a pp. 6 – 7; Marshall 2015b pp. 43 - 46). The Illuminati can ONLY activate a person's _REM driven_ clone when the person enters R.E.M sleep; usually about an hour and a half to two hours into sleeping. The Illuminati press a button [on a remote control] at the cloning center once the person is fully into REM sleep (when the original (real) person is asleep in her / his bed at home) and the person's consciousness is transferred, and the person opens up her / his eyes at the cloning center as a _REM driven_ clone version of themselves. People usually think they have been kidnapped for a second then they remember "Oh I'm just a _REM driven_ clone at the cloning center"... and that they are stuck there until they wake up _in their original body_. The Illuminati used the reality of REM driven cloning for the movie _A Nightmare on Elm Street_ (1984). The reality _of REM driven clones_ is: when you wake up _in your original body_ your _REM driven_ clone goes limp at the cloning center and falls to the floor. It goes "limp noodle". <u>**April 11, 2012 at 7:18pm**</u>

Why Donald Marshall can talk publicly about the Illuminati after visiting the cloning center

3SG1: How come the Illuminati let you go out from the cloning center each time you have been there; if the Illuminati know you tell the public what is going on at the cloning centers? Are the Illuminati that sure nobody will believe you so they take that risk?

DM: OK. That is easily explained. I am an original human being when I am awake and I experience life through my original, natural born body when I am awake. When I sleep and reach REM sleep my consciousness is transferred from my original body to my _REM driven_ clone, and then my _REM driven_ clone 'comes to life' because it now operates with my consciousness. When I wake up from sleeping, I am conscious in my original, natural born body, and experience life through my original body, and this is why I can talk about the Illuminati and all that they do. The real me is at a location far from the cloning center; and my _REM driven_ clone is at a location far from where my original body sleeps; furthermore, my _REM driven_ clone needs my consciousness (an original person's consciousness) to 'come to life'. I am **not** a replicated clone (i.e. a clone grown from a baby), entering and exiting the cloning center through physical movement.

DM: There are two bodies in this narrative. My original body, the one I was born with, and my *REM driven duplicate* clone bodies; for which *REM driven* duplicate clone bodies operate on REM driven consciousness / frequency. Moreover, *REM driven* duplicate clone bodies are clone bodies which the Illuminati grows by obtaining the DNA from an original, and growing duplicated clone bodies through the process of regenerative science, medicine and technology (i.e. stimulating the blood cells of an original person over and over again, until a fully formed human body of the original is grown; Science Channel 2014). Furthermore, the ONLY way the Illuminati can activate a person's *REM driven* clone is when the original's body is in R.E.M (rapid eye movement) sleep. A green light is displayed on a machine at the cloning center, alerting the Illuminati to the fact that a person's original body is now in REM sleep, and the Illuminati can transfer the person's consciousness to their *REM driven* clone duplicate stored at the cloning center. The Illuminati push a button, once the person is fully into REM sleep in their original body *(usually 90 -110 minutes after first falling asleep)*; the consciousness gets transferred to their *REM driven* clone at the cloning center and the person then opens their eyes as a *REM driven* clone at the cloning center, like *Boom* and people usually think they have been kidnapped. When a person's original body wakes up from sleep, or that person is woken up by someone else while sleeping, or something wakes that person up from sleep while she / he is a *REM driven* clone at the cloning center, her / his *REM driven* clone goes "limp noodle; as if dead.

REM driven cloning; duplication cloning; and replication cloning explained

DM: Moreover, REM cloning is achieved by a method called "Duplication cloning". Furthermore, REM driven cloning is **NOT** "Replication cloning". Replication cloning is the process of cloning an original person where the clone of the original person starts life off again as a baby, but replication cloning is an entirely different entity. There is no need for REM activation; the replicated clone (cloning from a baby up) will always be "on" – and replicated clones are genetic copies of original people in every way. Duplication cloning on the other hand makes a fully formed clone of a person. Are you 25 years old? You will have a 25 year old duplicate body for the Illuminati to do with as they want for 6-8 hours *(while you sleep in your original body, and your consciousness gets transferred to your REM driven clone duplicate)*. The Illuminati also makes multiple *duplicate REM driven* clones, and go through them (torture, sex, death spectacles etc.) one by one. It takes approximately five months through the process of regenerative medicine, science and technology *(by stimulating tissues and agitating them again and again)* to grow a human body this way. The duplicate clone bodies sometimes end up being deformed. Deformed duplicate clones do not matter to the Illuminati; the Illuminati just scrap those duplicate clone bodies, and start again. It hardly costs anything to grow duplicate clone bodies because the Illuminati have perfected the process of growing duplicate clone bodies, and therefore it is very cheap to produce one unit of output (a duplicate clone body). It is just maintenance of the duplicate clones after the five months when the duplicate clones have fully formed, which incurs costs. The Illuminati have these duplicate clone bodies stacked 2 by 2 (one duplicate clone body on top of another in containers) in a warehouse like room. I have seen it *as a REM driven clone* at the cloning center firsthand. Half formed duplicate clones look like 'demons' and half formed duplicate clones are horrifying to look at. I hope I have clarified that for you. Is there anything else you are wondering about? P.S. Spread the truth about these slimes *(about REM driven cloning and the Illuminati)* as far as you can please. **April 22, 2012 at 6:38pm**

The real Donald Marshall is not with the Illuminati members physically

3SG1: It makes more sense now why you can talk about them [the real you *(your original body)* is not with the Illuminati members physically, so when you wake up from having your consciousness transferred to your *REM driven* clone during sleep, and you remember what the Illuminati members said and did as *REM driven* clones, the real you can document it, and tell it to the world]. It does take them more effort to kill you since they are not there with you physically [the Illuminati members would have to kill the real you by torturing your *REM driven* clones for hours constantly before it kills the real you *(your original body)* because you are not with the Illuminati members physically]. Also, you are known now, so you are almost in Phase Two. You blasted up fast in the truther conversations. You will be a threat if dead, for sure.

DM: I am sick right now [from *REM driven* clone torture *of my REM driven clones* at the cloning center]. I have got to lay down on my back now and NOT SLEEP. I feel terrible. However, I will make a video when I am home. I feel like I am going to cry right now. I have to get out of the cloning centers permanently. I will be uploading a video when I have calmed down, and I am in a Wi-Fi spot. Keep helping by spreading the word on the Illuminati's REM driven cloning subculture. I am literally begging you... keep helping by spreading the word about the Illuminati's REM driven cloning subculture while I am gone [have left the library]. Make this poor unfortunate soul a priority in your life... help me save the world, by informing the world about the Illuminati's REM driven cloning subculture. What is the title of the album by Megadeth (2001) that I am on? I am just wondering if you know [what the Megadeth album (2001) that I am on is called?]. Look it up if you do not know. Time is in short supply for me, I fear. **May 14, 2012 at 9:11pm** ·

The title of the Megadeth album referenced is called "The World Needs A Hero"

The reality of REM driven cloning

3SG1: OH my God! I understand and must say for me REM driven cloning is not simple. This is horrible!

DM: This situation *(REM driven cloning and the Illuminati)* is horrible, and it is even worse to witness it firsthand hand than to read it on paper or imagine it. The Illuminati people and the *REM driven* clones at the cloning center, actually LIKE watching children die: *REM driven* clone children, as well as real children who are brought to the cloning centers; these Illuminati people actually LIKE watching children die. The Illuminati members also like watching adults die *(REM driven* clones of adults as well as real adults who are brought to the cloning centers *in their original bodies)*. The Illuminati members like to watch the life fade from children's eyes –just before a child dies *(REM driven clone children, as well as, real children, brought to the cloning centers in their original bodies)*. The Illuminati members also like watching the life fade from the eyes of adults as they die *(also REM driven clone adults and real adults who are brought to the cloning centers in their original bodies)*.

DM: Furthermore, the Illuminati *members, as REM driven clones at the cloning center* watch these deaths, of *REM driven* clones and real people (brought to the cloning center *in their original bodies*) and masturbate to their deaths. I am SO SORRY to sound crude, SERIOUSLY, but that is what the Illuminati do. Some of the *REM driven* clones at the cloning center, think it is a terrible nightmare. However, these people *as REM driven clone versions of themselves* will not voice their opinion for fear of reprisal, but I will. **April 22, 2012 at 7:19pm ·**

3SG1: I know about the [human] sacrifices. I read a lot and [human] sacrifices have been going on for centuries. Human sacrifice is so horrible to think about. I feel so much pain.

DM: It is distressing to know humans could treat other humans this way. I can only tell the world what I know and have witnessed firsthand *(through the process of consciousness transfer to my REM driven clone)*. Keep spreading the truth about *REM driven* cloning and the Illuminati. **April 22, 2012 at 7:23pm**

REM driven clone activation and distance

3SG1: Can't you run away so that the Illuminati can't find you? Somehow? It must be possible; you can't live like this anymore!

DM: No. There is no distance limit to this *REM driven* cloning technology. I could travel to Australia (I'm in Canada now) and the Illuminati could just push a button at the cloning center whenever I enter REM sleep, and my consciousness will still be transferred *from my original body (which lies in bed asleep in Australia)* to my *REM driven* clone at the cloning center in Canada. This *REM driven* cloning situation is not good. I have to get out of the cloning centers permanently. **April 22, 2012 at 7:23pm**

The Illuminati members do NOT use a teleportation device to travel to the cloning center

3SG1: Do they [the Illuminati members] have a teleportation device? How do they make time to travel back and forth [to the cloning center]?

3SG2: 3SG1, these are just cloned bodies that Donald is speaking of. The cloned bodies of *original* people are located at the cloning centers. When *original* people enter REM sleep [*90 -110 minutes after first falling asleep*] their consciousness is transferred to their cloned bodies, and the cloned bodies then become capable of movement, but the *original* people are still asleep in their own beds. Think "Avatar" (2009).

How Donald Marshall gets to the cloning center from home

3SG1: I have read about Tila Tequila in the past. Tila Tequila tried to turn against them and they punished her! So when you fall asleep, do you automatically go there? How do you get to the cloning center from your home? God, it is awful!

DM: A person's original (real) body stays asleep in their bed. Through the process of consciousness transfer, a person's consciousness is transferred by the Illuminati once the person reaches REM stage of sleep *(which is approximately 90-110 minutes after first falling asleep)*, from their original (real) body which lays in bed asleep, to their *REM driven* clone located at a remote location here on 3D physical earth, and the person then opens their *REM driven* clone eyes at a remote location far away from where they are sleeping (the cloning center). When a person wakes up from sleeping in real life their *REM driven* clone drops limp at the cloning center, because an original person's consciousness overrides the consciousness of a *REM driven* clone. When a person goes to sleep the next night, and the person reaches REM sleep, the Illuminati transfers that person's consciousness to their *REM* clone located at the cloning center the following night. It's as easy as that. **May 15, 2012 at 6:50pm ·**

The effects of REM driven clone torture on a person's original (real) body

The side effects of REM driven clone torture

3SG1: When you say you are being tortured, do you mean your [REM driven] clone is being tortured?

DM: Yes, the Illuminati are only torturing my [REM driven] clone but it gives me side effects in my original body because consciousness is linked (see Ehrsson 2013, for a demonstration on consciousness transfer and how consciousness is linked). *REM driven* clone torture causes different side effects for different people. *REM driven* clone torture damages a person's heart if the torture of the person's *REM driven* clone(s) is carried out consistently. It will cause the person to have an aneurysm or heart attack in their original body the next day (because consciousness is linked; Petkova and Ehrsson 2008; Ehrsson 2013). The Illuminati monitor my vital signs at the cloning center and keep my heart on the brink of a heart attack *(in my original body)*... they keep their torture just on the brink of giving me a heart attack *in my original body*. The Illuminati torture me just enough not to kill me *in my original body*. The intermittent torture over the years has messed up my heart *in my original body* badly now. I am healthy everywhere else, but I have only just started showing all the early warning signs for a stroke, and I am only 36. The Illuminati are getting more confident because there is no global panic or riots or masses of people demanding polygraph tests to get to the bottom of this. Because people are not spreading these truths about the Illuminati in their thousands, the Illuminati have renewed the torture of my *REM driven* clones at the cloning center. The Illuminati have began their torture of my *REM driven* clones at the cloning center harshly now, to show the other *REM driven* clones at the cloning center that this is what will happen to you if you start talking about *REM driven* clones and human cloning publicly... I could barely make it to the library to message on Facebook today... because I am feeling so weak *in my original body*.

DM: I am getting sicker *in my original body* from *REM driven* clone torture at the cloning center. Spread the letter (Donald Marshall Proboards 2012), spread the Full Disclosure book on REM driven cloning (Marshall 2015b), spread the Summary Disclosure (Marshall 2015a), spread all my disclosures documents which disclose the nefarious deeds and secrets of the Illuminati; "like" and "share" my Facebook posts; spreading my disclosures are the only thing which is going to save me from the Illuminati. **April 11, 2012 at 7:18pm**

Dying as a REM driven clone, and dying in a person's natural born original body

3SG1: Donald, how are you not dead from beatings? I do not understand this...

DM: It takes hours of constant torture of multiple *REM driven* clones of a person to kill a person until the point the person is dead *in their original body (in real life)*...When a person dies as a *REM driven* clone, for example, dying in *REM driven* clone body one; the person's consciousness is then transferred by the Illuminati to another *REM driven* clone body (*REM driven* clone body two); and then another, and then another and then another and so on for many hours until the person dies of a heart attack or aneurysm *in their original (real) body (in real life)* from the constant torture of their multiple *REM driven* clones, and their consciousness registering the pain of each *REM driven* clone torture, because consciousness is linked (Petkova and Ehrsson 2008; Ehrsson 2013). Therefore, constant torture of a person's multiple *REM driven* clones over a prolonged period of time will kill a person *in their original body*, because consciousness is linked (Petkova and Ehrsson 2008; Ehrsson 2013). The description above is what it means to be "Mega-deathed" [different from the band name "Megadeth"] –constant, unrelenting torture of a person's *REM driven* clones. *As REM driven clone versions themselves*, the Illuminati members, had to cut up multiple guts of *REM driven* clone's belonging to Bernie Mac; the Illuminati *REM driven clones*, cut the guts of multiple *REM driven* clones which belonged to Bernie Mac, and later transferred Bernie Mac's consciousness to the next *REM driven* clone; next *REM driven* clone; next *REM driven* clone, and so on, for four or five hours approximately, as the Illuminati *REM driven clones* continuously cut the guts of each *REM driven* clone version of Bernie Mac. Furthermore, because consciousness is linked, and Bernie Mac's consciousness was registering the accumulated pain of each *REM driven* clone torture, the constant and unrelenting torture of Bernie Mac's *REM driven* clones over a four or five hour span continuously, caused Bernie Mac to die from an aneurysm *in his original (real) body* the next day, because consciousness is linked (Petkova and Ehrsson 2008; Ehrsson 2013).

With me, the Illuminati *REM driven clones* torture my *REM driven* clones for half an hour at a time at the cloning centers; then the Illuminati *REM driven clones* talk to me for a while *as REM driven clones at the cloning centers*; then back to hurting *REM driven* clones of me; then back to talking *as REM driven clones at the cloning center;* then it is "Make a song and you will get no more torture [*as REM driven clones at the cloning center*]" and I make them... You would make the songs too if it stopped you from getting tortured *as a REM driven clone*... ever heard of Nazi tooth torture? It is not good. I think the Illuminati *REM driven clones* are just trying to make me think that they are not concerned with the spread of the letter, but they are; they are frantic... and tell me *as REM driven clones* at the cloning center that when I make Document2 the Illuminati may have to kill me *(my original body)*. **April 25, 2012 at 5:49pm**

The differences between replicated clones and duplicate clones

Differences explained: Torturing replicated clones versus torturing duplicate clones

3SG1: If you clone a sheep, and the torture the cloned sheep, the *original (real)* sheep is not going to feel it. Donald, you do know that the autopsy on Bernie Mac confirmed something else?

3SG2: Bernie Mac died from pneumonia (fluid in the lungs) that was complicated by sarcoidosis that was in remission... not that I am discounting your story, Donald. Only that you have some of your information wrong. Maybe Bernie Mac stood up to them because he knew he was on his way out already? Or pneumonia was the result of him being tortured [*as REM driven clones*]. Which if that is the case, I would have to suspect his clone to have been subjected to torture relating to his lungs?

3SG2: In response to 3SG1's comment about the cloning and torture of sheep: this is a different kind of cloning. What you described was: "replication cloning", and yes, in that case the *original (real)* sheep would **not** feel the torture. This is duplication cloning. Think "Avatar" (2009). These *REM driven* clones are empty shells. The Illuminati can and do transfer peoples' consciousnesses into clone versions of themselves. Often clones are grown with implants already in place; which is why, later; when doctors occasionally discover the implants they cannot fathom how the implants got there. In this case, one is not being merely transferring into a new identical copy of oneself but rather, this is only occurring while one is asleep [REM driven cloning –as depicted in the movie *Avatar* (2009)]. Think of it like a person who is able to astral travel, but instead of just floating around and returning to her / his body later, the person is drawn to a different body that is a copy of themselves and inhabiting it temporarily. This is all completely plausible based on insider information that I am aware of. The celebrities, and most likely everyone there [at the cloning centers] is operating cloned copies of themselves. This [REM driven cloning technology] is being used to imprint prominent people with ideas and graphic experiences; to push their limits and test their reactions; to profile their character and manipulate it. This [REM driven cloning technology] is a way of controlling information that goes into popular songs and movies and influence business decisions. Most are not aware of what takes place when back in their normal life but they retain some of it [their REM driven cloning experiences] ...such as song lyrics. Legal exposure does not appear to be a risk to them [the Illuminati], because there is no real link that can be drawn between these people and this alternate clone night life which they lead. These people that are there are not there by choice ...as evident that many are seen by Don to be crying and averting their eyes or reluctant to participate. I think after awhile some may choose to be there but I don't think they had much of a choice prior unless they were approached in real life to obtain a DNA sample and agreed in some form. Those that grow to like it are "turned" so to speak and "become" one of them.

DM: 3SG2, you sound like you already know about *REM driven* cloning. You are almost exactly correct in your description. Different people suffer different side effects from *REM driven* clone torture. The most common side effect is heart trouble, which is what I suffer with *(from REM driven clone torture)*. Other side effects include symptoms which are similar to experiencing Asperger Syndrome (Medical News Today 2015b) or Attention Deficit Hyperactivity Disorder (ADHD) (Medical News Today 2015a) as well as many different side effects. With some people their liver quivers as a side effect resulting from *REM driven* clone torture; the Illuminati even put the fact that someone peoples' liver quivers as a direct result from *REM driven* clone torture in a song somewhere. The Illuminati can mess with people in many different ways. **April 26, 2012 at 7:46pm**

How the original (real) Donald Marshall is threatened

3SG1: How is Donald threatened if he [the original him / real him] is not the clone that is actually at the cloning center?

DM: The *REM driven* clone may not be my *actual (original)* body, however it is my consciousness which runs the *REM driven* clone. Furthermore, consciousness is linked; therefore, I display physiological and biological responses in my real body too when my *REM driven* clone is threatened because consciousness is linked (Petkova and Ehrsson 2008; Ehrsson 2013). Accordingly, intermittent *REM driven* clone torture damages a person's heart slowly over time because the person's consciousness records it in their actual body as if the torture was actually happening to their actual body. There are other side effects of intermittent *REM driven* clone torture, however, the biggest side effect for me, is heart damage. If a person's *REM driven* clones are continually tortured without respite, while the *original* person who has had their consciousness transferred to their *REM driven* clone(s) is asleep, then that person will either die in their sleep from an aneurysm or heart attack, or will die the next day if the person does manage to wake up from sleep because their consciousness will have recorded all the pain they suffered as a *REM driven* clone, because consciousness is linked. It takes a longer period of time to kill a young person through the process of torturing a young person's *REM driven* clones, before a young person will die in their actual body of a heart attack or aneurysm. **May 14, 2012 at 7:18pm**

Cloned celebrities, Media and Popular Culture

3SG1: I still do not understand. If the celebrities are cloned, is the clone what WE [as the public] see on TV and in the papers? For example, you mentioned Tila Tequila is a sex slave, so does she stay at the cloning center giving them sex, while her clone is out in public and that is what WE see on TV and in the papers? Is that right?! I am confused.

3SG2: That is what I wondered too. The celebrities we see on TV are they real people or clones of real people? I think the clones get tortured, am I right?

DM: I think the confusion may be due to the difference in replication cloning and duplication cloning. Replication cloning is growing a clone of an original, where the clone is an identical copy of an original and starts life off from a baby. Duplication cloning on the other hand happens from agitating the cells of an original over and over again until a fully formed duplicate clone of an original person is formed. It takes five months to grow a human body through the process of duplication cloning.

DM: REM driven cloning is a process which involves duplication cloning. Once the duplicate clones have formed completely into a human body, REM driven duplicate clones do not function unless, the consciousness of the original is transferred into the REM driven clone when the original person is in REM sleep *(90 – 110 minutes after first falling asleep)*; the *REM driven* clone comes to life once the consciousness of an original IN REM sleep resides in the *REM driven* clone as the original sleeps in their bed; once the original person wakes up from sleep, the REM driven clone drops limp –as if dead at the remote location (cloning centers). Therefore, Tila Tequila is a *REM driven* clone sex slave WHEN her original body is asleep; during the point where Tila Tequila reaches REM sleep, her consciousness is transferred to her *REM driven* clone at the cloning center, where THE *REM driven* clone *(Tila Tequila's REM driven clone)* comes to life because it now has Tila Tequila's consciousness running the *REM driven* clone, and therefore Tila Tequila as a *REM driven* clone version of herself, has to have sex with other *REM driven* clones in exchange for *the original (real)* Tila Tequila *(who is asleep in her bed)* to receive fame and promotions in real life, when she wakes up. As you can see it is very advanced science and technology...and this is how advanced science and technology is today.

If you are wondering whether you have seen clones on TV, whereby in the example above, *the original (real)* Tila Tequila is actually asleep and her consciousness has been transferred to her *REM driven* clone, and she is having sex at the cloning center as a *REM driven* clone version of herself, then the answer to that is also yes. *The original (real)* Tila Tequila, would be asleep in her bed, while as a *REM driven* clone version of herself she is having sex at the cloning center, while a DIFFERENT clone of Tila Tequila is shown TV; OR in this example the real Tila Tequila stays at home awake; she is not asleep having *REM driven* clone sex, but a clone version of herself is shown on TV.

So in short: Yes sometimes the people you see on TV are clones... and yes Tila Tequila has a *REM driven* clone duplicate of herself, whereby *the original (real)* Tila Tequila's consciousness is transferred whenever *the original (real)* Tila Tequila enters REM sleep *(90-110 minutes after first falling asleep)* and then Tila Tequila has sex (clone sex) as a *REM driven* clone of herself at the cloning center with Illuminati *REM driven* clones, in exchange for a TV show and fame (in real life). **May 15, 2012 at 8:09pm ·**

3SG1: Thank you.

REM driven cloning and fame

3SG2: So, when do these people realise they are going to be cloned? Do they realise they are going to be cloned when they become famous or just before they become famous? You said greed overtakes them!

DM: Yes, greed does overtake them. No, they do not realise they are going to be cloned, and will have to attend the cloning center as a *REM driven* clone version of themselves when they go sleep *(through the process of consciousness transfer from their original bodies to their REM driven clone located at the cloning center each time they fall into REM sleep in their original bodies).*

DM: Once they become famous they are allowed to participate in the Illuminati's REM driven cloning subculture and retain (some) memories (although they are told anything other than they are *REM driven* clone versions of themselves while they are asleep, such as: they are in the fifth dimension, quantum hopping, a singularity, the astral realm, Valhalla etc.) and then they attend the cloning centers as *REM driven* clone versions of themselves whenever they sleep, in order to get familiar with the Illuminati's REM driven cloning subculture, overtime. **May 15, 2012 at 10:10pm ·**

Why setting an alarm to avoid REM sleep and REM driven clone activation does not work.

3SG1: Donald, how about setting an alarm so that you wake up just before you hit REM sleep?

DM: I have done the alarm thing. It takes approximately one and a half hours to two hours to fully enter REM sleep after falling asleep. I have set the alarm for one hour after falling asleep before for many days. However, what happens when a person does that is that they become sick because the body needs REM sleep to survive. Once the body becomes exhausted from missing REM sleep, a person will not wake up to the alarm, and will sleep through the sound of their alarm... when this happens you sleep for longer hours and it feels like days spent at the cloning center as a *REM driven* clone... time feels like it is going really slowly at the cloning center (although time ticks just the same at the cloning centers as it does when you are awake *in your original body*) and I just pray to wake up *in my original body* soon, so that my *REM driven* clone can drop limp noodle at the cloning center, and I no longer have to be there *as a REM driven clone*. *REM driven* clone torture hurts badly. I am frantic... very frantic now... My health is getting worse and I was an athlete. I am 36, and they are slowly killing me with this intermittent *REM driven* clone torture when I sleep. I must tell the world about REM driven cloning, as well as, all the heinous crimes the Illuminati commits against humanity. It is my duty as a human being to tell the world about these crimes. I also want justice and vengeance for everything the Illuminati has done to me and my health, just so that losers like Justin Timberlake can have a new album. God save me from this [technologically driven nightmare], loan me the strength to soldier on and inform the good people of this world about what is going on right under their very noses with their own children and other insidious and nefarious acts. I will explain everything about the Illuminati. Everything. But I need more ears and more eyes. This must go **GLOBAL** or I am going to die *(in my original body)* from the intermittent *REM driven* clone torture carried out on my *REM driven* clones at the cloning center. **April 12, 2012 at 11:25pm**

3SG1: Donald, why don't you set an alarm so that you avoid REM sleep?

3SG2: Donald has mentioned that you die without REM sleep.

WHERE is the "HARD evidence" for human cloning / REM driven cloning?

Currently, evidence for human cloning / REM driven cloning is "Circumstantial evidence"

3SG1: Where is the evidence [for human cloning / REM driven cloning]?

DM: 3SG1, REM driven cloning is a fact of life and everything I am disclosing is all true; most people now know it is true, why don't you? I have told you my nephew will be speaking out against the Illuminati too, but he will do it at a more appropriate time. I am asking the public to demand that I, and other low level Illuminati members and then high rank Illuminati members, submit to polygraph tests. I am also constructing Document2 which will be so long that it will take days to complete with my limited library computer access. Document2 will contain the names of everyone I have ever seen at the cloning centers as *REM driven* clones; what these people have done at the cloning center as *their REM driven* clone duplicates, as well as, what these people have done to other REM driven clones; I will also detail insider information of what these people have done in real life; and I will also include other things the people mentioned in the upcoming Document2 have done. I will also mention the highly advanced technologies the Illuminati currently have, **available today**, hidden and in secret, as well as, all the weird stuff the Illuminati do... other than that what else CAN I do?!

I am a poor 36 year old man with no connections against the richest and most powerful people in this world; trapped as a *REM driven* clone, in the biggest most powerful corrupt cult the world has ever seen. I have no choice but to inform the world about the Illuminati REM driven cloning subculture and all that I have seen them do, firsthand. They are torturing my *REM driven* clones almost daily; you would understand if the Illuminati *REM driven clones at the cloning center* stabbed a *REM driven* clone of you just ONCE! I have no choice but to inform the world about the Illuminati REM driven cloning subculture; the ONLY thing the Illuminati members fear is the populace learning about their REM driven cloning subculture and demanding Illuminati members submit to polygraph tests. The police and Royal Canadian Mounted Police (RCMP) high ups all have *REM driven* clone duplicates and attend the cloning center; the police and RCMP are loyal to The Crown (the British Monarchy)... someone help me. It is true. It is all true, and there is much more... it will be a long letter; just the names alone will be pages long; but I will make sure the populace knows everything that I know about the Illuminati; the Illuminati's REM driven cloning subculture and everything I have seen the Illuminati do firsthand. It is a lot of content. Just the Illuminati's complicity alone in the Robert Pickton murders should bring the Illuminati to complete ruin.

The mentality of the Illuminati members and the Illuminati's better technological advantage

DM: During the Robert Pickton murders, a few rich people visited Robert Pickton's house and ate some pieces of the dead prostitutes on a barbeque. These rich people wanted to see what human flesh, REAL human flesh (and not cloned humans) taste like; because loyal Illuminati members have it **ingrained** into their heads that: "To be evil is cool". Therefore, the nerds walk around trying to talk like Gothic Vampires; acting all dark and mysterious and going about life committing evil deeds.

They are rich and politically powerful, cowardly nerdy perverts, hiding in the shadows and messing with *(REM driven)* cloned people and children *(real children and REM driven clones of children)*. Messing with people makes the Illuminati members feel 'powerful'... in the respect that these members will proclaim "Oooohhh... I'm an evil slave-master" –that is their mentality. However, the reality of the situation is that it is just a technological advantage *(REM driven cloning)* which the Illuminati uses against an unsuspecting populace. Moreover, because the Illuminati have better technological advantages in comparison to what we the populace use, there is currently no defence against REM driven cloning, and no defence against the other technologies which they have and use against the populace, because it is a **technological advantage** which the Illuminati hold.

Technological advantages allow the Illuminati to escape detection with "Hard evidence"

DM: There is also no way for the Illuminati to get caught in the respect of demonstrating human cloning and REM driven cloning with "hard evidence" currently; because the Illuminati hold many technological advantages, as well as, better technological advantages in comparison to what we the populace use; and as a direct result the Illuminati have covered many bases to ensure that they are not caught. However, the circumstantial evidence is ALL around you. REM driven cloning is a fact of life and currently exists. REM driven cloning, as well as many of highly advanced technologies which I have seen firsthand and I will be disclosing, are real; a fact of life; and currently exist **today**. The technology exists today; not in five years from now; ten; twenty or a hundred years from now; the technologies I discuss exist today! Seriously, these highly advanced technologies, REM driven cloning and more exist today and are present at the cloning centers. The cloning centers are a paedophile's paradise and it must be stopped! Seriously! The cloning centers ARE a paedophile's paradise and it MUST be stopped! If I die writing Document2, continue to spread awareness about REM driven cloning guys. The populace learning about REM driven cloning is the world's only hope against the Illuminati's better technological advantages. Seriously! There highest authority is the populace.

REM driven cloning is the main topic which TRULY exposes the Illuminati

DM: Therefore it is in the populaces' best interest to learn and understand everything I will be disclosing from my eyewitness accounts *(at the cloning centers as a REM driven clone)*, which was CLEARLY proven to me as fact regarding the Illuminati's highly technological advantages, which include REM driven cloning and more. Informing the populace about the TRUE nature of the Illuminati and their REM driven cloning subculture to the point where a large percent of the world's population understand REM driven cloning and what the Illuminati members REALLY do, and how they do it, is what TRULY will expose the Illuminati and set forth a chain reaction towards the Illuminati's complete downfall. The populace demanding answers and polygraph tests about cloning, human cloning and REM driven cloning, as well as, everything the Illuminati members do, and have done, is what is going to TRULY expose the Illuminati.

Therefore, it is in the populace's best interest to start talking about cloning, human cloning, and the Illuminati's REM driven cloning subculture, and what the Illuminati members have done as REM driven clones and in real life, and keep spreading the word; keep informing more and more of the populace about these topics. REM driven cloning is what exposes the Illuminati.

I know my statements sound heavy, but it is true. This time an insider with valuable information is actually telling the populace the complete truth and providing the populace with knowledge the populace can use to defend itself against the biggest most powerful corrupt cult the world has ever seen. This is the time to defeat them. Do something soon or be slaves to the Illuminati forever. The Illuminati can clone almost anyone. However, people with "Riley-Day Syndrome" (medically known as: Familial dysautonomia (FD)) (Medline Plus 2016) cannot be cloned for some reason, and I wish I had that syndrome. **April 26, 2012 at 7:46pm**

The differences between "dreams" and "REM driven clone activation"

3SG1: So how does Donald know that it is not his beliefs influencing his dreams?

DM: A *REM driven* clone experience is not like dreams. I haven't had a dream or nightmare in years. Having *REM driven* clone experiences stops a person from having a dream or nightmare for the night; the person will just walk and talk as a *REM driven* clone version of themselves and experience the same earth the person left behind when he or she went to sleep. Furthermore, *REM driven* clone experiences are not like dreaming, dreams are fuzzy and incoherent. When I open my eyes as a *REM driven* clone it is **CLEAR**, clear like I am talking to you now; and when I am just about to wake up *in my original body*, my *REM driven* clone drops "limp noodle" –as if dead *(the REM driven clone at the cloning center)* and my consciousness goes from remembering an experience here on earth, CLEAR as daylight, at a remote location (the cloning centers), to a moment lasting about a second or two of blurriness before I open eyes *in original body* to experience the world again, only this time in my original body, CLEAR as daylight! That is consciousness transfer and how it feels to be a *REM driven* clone explained. A person is LITERALLY waking up as a clone, to experience the same world they left behind when their original (real) body went to sleep. **May 14, 2012 at 7:18pm**

REM driven cloning is CLEAR as daylight and does NOT feel like "an awful nightmare"

3SG2: Wow! So it is scary to go to sleep then? The less time you sleep the better. So does [REM driven clone experiences] it feel like an awful nightmare while you are sleeping?

DM: No. Absolutely not! Dreams and nightmares are fuzzy... and sometimes a person is not even aware that they are in fact dreaming or had a dream while they went to sleep. With consciousness transfer to a *REM driven* clone, the experience is CLEAR as daylight, and a person experiences the same earth that person left behind when her or his original (real) body went to sleep; only this time the person is experiencing the same earth as a *REM driven* clone version of herself or himself.

As a *REM driven* clone, a person also walks around the earth, and talks exactly the same, experiencing the same earth, CLEAR as daylight, exactly AS IF the person was experiencing life in their original body. Time, and minutes pass just the same as a *REM driven* clone as it does when a person is awake *in original body (because a person is experiencing the same earth, only this time, as a REM driven clone version of themselves, instead of in their original body).* The sequence of events as *REM driven* clone is also linear, and the sequence of events are **NOT** non-linear, such as dreams and nightmares. When a person wakes up from sleep their *REM driven* clone goes limp and drops because the consciousness of an original (real) person overrides the consciousness of a *REM driven* clone, as well as the fact that a *REM driven* clone needs the consciousness of an original to function. However, the CLARITY is one of the worst things of being a *REM driven* clone. The experience of being a *REM driven* clone is SO CLEAR (like I am talking to you now). The others who attend the cloning centers as REM driven clone versions of themselves, sacrifice their ability to dream and have nightmares in exchange to attend the cloning center as a *REM driven* clone version of themselves. A person sacrifices his or her ability to dream or have a nightmare for the night, because when a person's consciousness is transferred to his or her REM driven clone, the consciousness transfer to the REM driven clone stops that person from having a dream or nightmare for the evening which the person went sleep. **May 15, 2012 at 7:44pm**

The original person, who sleeps, controls the actions of the REM driven clone

3SG1: So when they [Illuminati members] are asleep do they control what their [REM driven] clones do, such as the torture [of other REM driven clones etc]? Do the Illuminati members real bodies suffer from *REM driven* cloning like Donald? How do they [Illuminati members] get enjoyment from it all whilst they are asleep?! Sick b******s!

3SG2: When the Illuminati members reach REM sleep *(90 -110 minutes after first falling asleep)* their consciousness can then be transferred into their *REM driven* clone body at the cloning center. The *REM driven* clone bodies are stored on steel racks, which contain five rows, with each row containing a *REM driven* clone body. Once an Illuminati member's consciousness is transferred to their *REM driven* clone at the cloning center, the *REM driven* clone comes to life and becomes "awake" at the cloning center. Yes, the Illuminati members control what their *REM driven* clones do.

3SG1: So they [Illuminati members] are aware of what they are doing, and they are also controlling the *REM driven* clone's actions? What if Donald wakes up?

3SG2: Yes... the Illuminati members are aware of what they are doing as *REM driven* clones. When Donald wakes up in his real body his *REM driven* clone drops "limp noodle" to the ground, as if dead at the cloning center, and his consciousness goes back to his real body.

DM: Exactly... and yes, the Illuminati members know everything they do as *REM driven* clones. A person knows exactly what he or she is doing as a *REM driven* clone unless that person is memory suppressed as a *REM driven* clone. In response to your question regarding "How do they get enjoyment from it all while asleep?" the answer is: The Illuminati members are just arrogant and thought they would never get caught. **May 14, 2012 at 9:06pm**

Do the same people attend the cloning centers?

3SG1: Do the same people attend the cloning center as *REM driven* clones versions of themselves every night? What if a person wants a night off, or does a person have to attend the cloning center as a *REM driven* clone version of themselves all the time?

DM: There are different people sometimes, who attend the above ground cloning center which I attend as a *REM driven* clone version of myself. When I fall asleep in the middle of the day for example, for a while I see all kinds of unfamiliar faces as *REM driven* clones *at the cloning center*. The Illuminati members try and sleep when I do so that they can be present at the cloning center as a *REM driven* clone version of themselves at the same time as I am activated as a *REM driven* clone. Some people have the choice NOT to be activated as a *REM driven* clone at the cloning center while they sleep, however, I do **not** have this choice. I am unwillingly activated as a *REM driven* clone at the cloning center whenever I sleep. The celebrities who are receiving benefits in real life HAVE to attend the cloning center as *REM driven* clones of themselves when they sleep. For example, with Tila Tequila: the Illuminati members are messing with Tila Tequila *(in real life and as a REM driven clone version of herself)* right now because she does not want to be a *REM driven* clone sex slave anymore to a bunch of old, fat, rich, bald guys as *REM driven* clone versions of themselves at the cloning center. The Illuminati members are messing with Tila Tequila almost every day, as well as, doing many other things to her. I do not have much sympathy for Tila Tequila; as a *REM driven* clone *version of herself*, Tila Tequila was very mean to me *as a REM driven clone version of myself at the cloning center.* **May 15, 2012 at 5:40pm**

Why Donald Marshall cannot fight back as a REM driven clone

3SG1: Hello Donald, I am new to your revelations but I have been reading about your ordeals all day and watching your videos. Forgive me for my ignorance, but in your clone state, are you unable to fight back? Surely you can disarm [Queen] Elizabeth [II] and slit her throat (sadistic b***h).

DM: One of the many functions of a *REM driven* clone which the Illuminati can control is the ability to paralyse a *REM driven* clone at the push of a button. The Illuminati have a button on a remote control, which they can push, for any *REM driven* clone (of the Illuminati's choice) to become paralysed (while the person's consciousness is intact in the REM driven clone); the *REM driven* clone then drops limp at the push of the button, on the remote control. Once when I was *a REM driven clone version of myself* at the cloning center, I faked being paralysed.... Queen Elizabeth II *as a REM driven clone version of herself* thought the programmer in the control room had paralysed me *when I was REM driven clone at the cloning center*, but I was not really paralysed *as a REM driven clone*; and therefore, *as a REM driven clone of myself* I jumped up and started smashing the pig in the face [Queen Elizabeth II *as a REM driven clone version of herself at the cloning center*]. It was strange to see an old looking hag getting knocked senseless, but that is exactly what I did in the past to Queen Elizabeth II *as a REM driven clone version of herself when I was a REM driven clone version of myself at the cloning center*. Unfortunately, *as a REM driven clone of herself,* Queen Elizabeth II had her pain sensors turned off in her *REM driven* clone body and her pain sensors were reduced to zero anyway.

Consequently, *as a REM driven clone of herself,* Queen Elizabeth II did not feel any pain even though *as a REM driven clone of myself,* I knocked Queen Elizabeth II senseless *when she was a REM driven clone of herself at the cloning center. As REM driven clone versions of themselves,* the Illuminati members can turn the pain sensors of *REM driven* clones off (to zero); this is another function which the Illuminati has on a remote control for *REM driven* clones. The Illuminati have the technology to turn the pain sensors off for *REM driven* clones, and consequently, make *REM driven* clones "pain numb" like quadriplegics but still ensure the *REM driven* clones are capable of movement (walking, running etc). **May 15, 2012 at 5:43pm** ·

3SG1: Jesus! It is a shame there is no way of creating an uprising with your fellow clones and getting into the mainframe for how they control [REM driven] clones. I know I am probably ignorant of the power [and technology] they wield, but I am desperate to find a way out of this nightmare for you... I shall keep reading and pray for you. Good luck sir.

Cloning Center

How Donald Marshall enters and leaves the cloning center

3SG1: How are you able to leave the Cloning Centers, when you could easily get them all in trouble?

DM: The Illuminati can **ONLY** activate a person's *REM driven* clone, when the person is REM sleep. They activate me as *REM driven* clones nearly every night, talking nonsense to me as *REM driven* clones, threatening me as *REM driven* clones, then begging me to stop talking about them as *REM driven* clones. Then they torture my *REM driven* clones and threaten to hurt my *REM driven* clone body until I have a heart attack or aneurysm *in my original body* while I am asleep. This is possible because consciousness is linked (Petkova and Ehrsson 2008; Ehrsson 2013), and therefore, when they inflict pain on my *REM driven* clone body, it affects my original body. The Illuminati members therefore threaten me *as REM driven clone versions,* that they are going to hurt me till I have a heart attack or aneurysm like they made Bernie Mac (actor / comedian) have an aneurysm *in his original body through the constant torture of his REM driven clones* –because consciousness is linked (Petkova and Ehrsson 2008; Ehrsson 2013). The Illuminati are frantic now and want to make me stop talking. However they do not want to kill me because they said I might be Jesus (which I am **NOT**) and if they killed me it might bring about the end of the world somehow through some prophecy... a bunch of stupid stuff... I HAVE to get the cloning stations shut down. Right now the only way is to tell people what the Illuminati do; as many people as possible. The Illuminati really did NOT like me telling the "Anonymous" people –you know- "Anonymous" –"We Are Legion". The people in Anonymous were overjoyed to meet me and cannot wait to meet me [again] and talk more. **April 5, 2012 at 3:43pm**

Donald Marshall discusses REM driven cloning with "Anonymous" We Are Legion

3SG1: Donald, have you met "Anonymous"? What did Anonymous say and why haven't they posted a video about your whistle blowing disclosure yet?

3SG2: No, Donald has NOT met "Anonymous". 99% of Anonymous has gone off-line and off the grid. Donald is speaking to the new wave of supporters.

DM: That's true [I haven't met "Anonymous"]... but many "Anonymous" people ("We Are Legion") are messaging me by email; just to say "Thank you", and "Thank God for you, and that kind of stuff..." **April 10, 2012 at 2:25pm**

Updates: Donald Marshall's REM driven cloning activation

3SG1: Donald, are you still be brought to the cloning centers?

DM: Yes... nearly every night. **April 10, 2012 at 2:54pm**

3SG1: Donald, this worries me, why isn't there somebody there helping you?

DM: Everyone who attends the cloning centers as *REM driven* clones, is scared. Anyone who speaks up for me gets yelled at and threatened by Queen Elizabeth II *as a REM driven clone,* or another loyal Illuminati member at the cloning center.

DM: After Bernie Mac was murdered from the cloning centers *(through the torture of Bernie Mac's REM driven clones –because consciousness is linked, and torturing a person's REM driven clones affects them in their original body)* nobody speaks up for me *as REM driven clones at the cloning center*. Everyone who attends the same cloning center *as REM driven clone versions of themselves*, that I unwillingly have my consciousness transferred to are afraid, and they are hoping I am successful at telling the world so they can escape *REM driven cloning and* the cloning centers too. They hope the Illuminati do not kill me *(in my original body)* before I reach a level of world attention... the Illuminati have turned up the heat on the torture of my *REM driven* clones there big time. The torture of my *REM driven* clones is making me sicker *in my original body* everyday now. Help me spread the letter [and all my disclosure documents please], it's the only thing that will save me... or I am doomed. Seriously. **April 11, 2012 at 7:22pm**

3SG1: Donald, are you still being brought to the cloning center?

DM: Queen Elizabeth II keeps transferring my consciousness *from my original body to my REM driven clone whenever I sleep and reach REM sleep (at home in my bed, 90-110 minutes after first falling asleep)* and activating my *REM driven* clone(s) stored at the cloning center. Queen Elizabeth II *as a REM driven clone of version of herself, at the cloning center* keeps talking foolishness to me *(when I am activated as a REM driven clone at the cloning center)* "Why Dun? We loff you Dun. Stay weeth oos Dun" [Why Don? We love you Don. Stay with us Don]. As a REM driven clone version of myself at the cloning center I just say to Queen Elizabeth II *(also a REM driven clone at the cloning center)* "Well, No!" "With all the torture you have carried out on me [*my REM driven clones at the cloning center*], you have ruined my life systematically. You tried to tell world of rich people [*who also attend the cloning centers as REM driven duplicates of themselves*] that I am "The Antichrist" and it is OK to torture me [*my REM driven clones at the cloning center*] to a slow death and God will love them more for it [*torturing clones of me*]".

"You had real children [*in their original bodies and not REM driven cloned children*] brought here [*the cloning centers*] and you executed these children and you watch the videos of the children being executed at the cloning center and you masturbate to the children's deaths". "You are not someone I would EVER want to be around or know Elizabeth. Now leave me alone. I do not want to make songs anymore [*as a REM driven clone at the cloning center*]" Then Queen Elizabeth II *as a REM driven clone of herself*, as well as, the other Illuminati members who are also *REM driven* clones at the cloning center, will cry. The Illuminati are retarded and must be stopped! **April 22, 2012 at 6:08pm ·**

Countries involved with REM driven cloning

3SG1: Donald, why don't you come to Australia? Is Australia involved with the cloning centers?

DM: I'd actually love to go to Australia. The leadership there is also involved with the Illuminati and the Australian leadership attend the cloning centers *as REM driven clone versions of themselves.* But when the leadership of Australia realized just how senile and crazy Queen Elizabeth II is *(as a REM driven clone at the cloning center)* Australia decided to declare independence from England finally. Australia declaring its independence happened somewhat recently, and it is directly because of the cloning centers. Australia does not like Queen Elizabeth II and does not want to be associated with Queen Elizabeth II that closely. I asked the Australian leaders who attend the cloning centers *as REM driven clones:* "Why don't they just boycott the cloning stations in Australia [and stop attending the cloning centers]?" The leadership of Australia said *(as REM driven clones at the cloning center)* "They [Australia] have to remain status quo and stay in the REM driven cloning / cloning centers business or Queen Elizabeth II or the economic vultures (loyal Illuminati members who want to keep REM driven cloning, and the cloning centers) will make the economic climate rain on Australia like they did to Greece." GREECE is **NOT** at the cloning centers. There are no Greek leaders who attend the cloning centers as *REM driven* clone versions of themselves. There are no Greek leaders at the cloning centers. As a consequence of boycotting the cloning centers Queen Elizabeth II CHOSE Greece to suffer economic troubles. Queen Elizabeth II made Greece suffer economic troubles to boost the economies for other countries that attend the cloning centers *as REM driven clone versions of themselves* and are loyal to Queen Elizabeth II. Seriously. I was there at the cloning center *as a REM driven clone* when this decision by Queen Elizabeth II against Greece was implemented. **April 12, 2012 at 6:02pm**

Where is the location of the cloning center?

3SG1: Where is this cloning center? Keep exposing people!

DM: Unknown. Most people who are activated as *REM driven* clones at the cloning center do not even know the location of the above ground cloning center in Canada... The cloning center *(which I unwillingly have my consciousness transferred to my REM driven clone whenever my original body enters REM sleep)*, looks like a small sports forum. Outside of this small sport-looking-forum, there is no civilisation around. There is grass and trees, which extends further out from the above ground, Canadian cloning center; then as far as the eye can see there is nothing... There is nobody nearby enough to hear screams... I am exposing many, many people who attend the cloning centers *as REM driven clones.* I am making a very long list of people who have attended the cloning center *as REM driven clones*, with footnotes included of what they do *as REM driven clones* at the cloning center. I will call it "Document 2". **April 12, 2012 at 6:38pm**

Why Donald Marshall has not stated the location of the cloning center

3SG1: So why don't you say the location [of the cloning center]?

DM: The location of the cloning center? OK. Well... even most of the willing Illuminati members who are *REM driven clone versions of themselves* at the cloning center do not know the location. They just get "cloned in" as they call it. The location of the cloning center is in the middle of nowhere and there is no civilisation in sight... If I knew the location of the cloning center, I would have said this by now... However the cloning center which I am activated *as a REM driven clone* is above ground and located somewhere in Canada... However, there are more than one cloning centers, worldwide. **May 9, 2012 at 9:03pm** ·

The reasons willing Illuminati members do NOT know the location of the cloning centers

3SG1: So, how would the willing members be able to get in and out without knowing the location?

DM: The willing members, have their consciousness transferred from their original bodies to their *REM driven* clone bodies located at the cloning center, when they go to sleep, and reach REM sleep *(90-110 minutes after first falling asleep in their original bodies)* and once their consciousness has been transferred to their *REM driven* clone, the willing members THEN "wake up" and open their eyes as a *REM driven* clone version of themselves at the cloning center. It is similar to the process depicted in the movie *Avatar* (2009). A *REM driven* clone can only become active while the original person's body is in REM sleep. The Illuminati keep the *REM driven* clone bodies on stainless steel racks, "on wait"... and once a person / a willingly member is in REM sleep, a green light is displayed on a machine, alerting the Illuminati to the fact that a person is now in REM sleep, and it is time to transfer the person's consciousness to their *REM driven* clone. Essentially, the *REM driven* clones are 'empty shells' and need the consciousness of an original to operate.

REM driven clones are kept in storage on the stainless steel racks at the cloning center and sleep like 'vampires'... waiting for their time to 'come alive'. Therefore, this is how a person can 'come in and out' of the cloning center and not know the location of the cloning center. The person "wakes up" as a *REM driven* clone version of themselves at the cloning center through the process of consciousness transfer; and the "high rank" Illuminati *REM driven* clones do not share the location of the cloning center with just anybody... even willing Illuminati members... **May 9, 2012 at 9:19pm** ·

REM driven cloning experiences happen in the 3D physical world and NOT the 'Astral Realm'

3SG1: Donald, are these experiences happening in the Astral [Realm], or physical?

DM: These *REM driven cloning* experiences are happening in the 3D physical world, through the process of consciousness transfer from my original body to my *REM driven* clone whenever I sleep (at home in bed) and enter REM sleep *(90-110 minutes after first falling asleep)*; a green light appears on a machine at the above ground cloning center *(located in Canada, within 5 / 6 hours drive of the Robert Pickton Farm)* to indicate to the Illuminati that I am now in REM sleep, and it is now time to transfer my consciousness.

Consciousness transfer *to a REM driven clone* is similar to that depicted in the movie *Avatar* (2009), as well as, *Inception* (2010) and when I wake up from the experience of being a *REM driven* clone I retain the full memories of the experiences because all my *REM driven clone* experiences have been released to me and I am no longer memory suppressed. Once the Illuminati releases a person's REM driven cloning experiences, the Illuminati cannot keep a person from remembering their *REM driven cloning* experiences when the Illuminati transfers that person's consciousness from their original body to the person's *REM driven* clone. The person will always remember the experience [when the person wakes up from sleeping in his / her original body].

How it feels to be a REM driven clone explained

DM: Furthermore, when the Illuminati transfer my consciousness to my *REM driven* clone, I open my eyes like *Boom* -and it feels like I have been kidnapped for a second, then I remember I am at the above ground cloning center in Canada. It is not like dreaming, dreams are fuzzy and incoherent. When I open my eyes as a *REM driven* clone it is **CLEAR**, clear like I am talking to you now; and when I am just about to wake up *in my original body*, my *REM driven* clone drops "limp noodle" -as if dead (the *REM driven* clone at the cloning center) and my consciousness goes from remembering an experience here on earth, CLEAR as daylight, at a remote location (the cloning centers), to a moment lasting about a second or two of blurriness before I open eyes in my original body to experience the world again, only this time in my original body, CLEAR as daylight! That is consciousness transfer and how it feels to be a *REM driven* clone explained. A person is LITERALLY waking up as a clone, to experience the same world they left behind when their original (real) body went to sleep. The side effects however, is that clones and REM driven clones are dumber; *REM driven* clones have a heightened sense of emotions and are more impulsive than the original experiencing the world in their original body.

Description of the above ground cloning center in Canada, A.K.A "The Diddle Dome"

DM: The cloning center is a physical location here on earth, and my *REM driven* clone experiences are happening in the 3D physical, here on earth. The above ground cloning center in Canada is a small sports arena, with a small dome. I call it "The Diddle Dome" and the Illuminati members hate it when I call the cloning centers "The Diddle Dome". The above ground cloning center in Canada is isolated and I do not know the location.

DM: However, Stephen Harper knows the location of the above ground cloning center located in Canada along with many high rank Illuminati members. However, half the Illuminati members who attend the cloning centers as *REM driven* clones do not know the exact location of the above ground cloning center in Canada; they just get "cloned in" as they call it. Steven Spielberg attends the above ground cloning center *as a REM driven clone of himself* and knows who I am. *As REM driven clones at the cloning center,* Steven Spielberg has discussed movies and told me stories at the cloning center. Moreover, because of all the songs I made from the cloning center *as a REM driven clone*, the Illuminati *REM driven clones* started to think I would be good at other things too; the song making generated interest in me and soon everyone wanted to meet me *as a REM driven clone at the cloning center*. Furthermore, *as REM driven clones at the cloning center*, if I couldn't help a certain person or give that person a good idea or story or song, then that person *as a REM driven clone of themselves* would literally torture me *as a REM driven clone* in various ways while other *REM driven* clones at the cloning center watched; some *REM driven* clones cried; some *REM driven* clones laughed; some *REM driven* clones masturbated as I was being tortured *as a REM driven clone* at the cloning center. REM driven cloning and the cloning centers are bad and someone HAS to do something! The Illuminati members do many evil things as *REM driven* clones at the cloning centers; the Illuminati members also commit many acts of evil in real life too, and record their evil deeds on video, to re-watch "the evil acts" as *REM driven* clones at the cloning center. Spread the truth about the Illuminati and their REM driven cloning subculture, as well as, all the evil the Illuminati perpetrates to the four corners of the earth. **April 27, 2012 at 7:59pm**

Possible outcomes when REM driven cloning gains worldwide attention

3SG1: Will they bring you to the cloning center when this is well known?

DM: True. The Illuminati will transfer my consciousness from my original body to my *REM driven* clone located at the above ground cloning center in Canada again when the confidence level rises. The Illuminati and the cloning centers must be shut down and the perpetrators who have committed crimes brought to justice. I want to see Queen Elizabeth II (the original and NOT ANY of her clones) answer to the world for what she's been doing and allowing others (Illuminati members) to do to the populace. **April 14, 2012 at 6:09pm**

Shut down of cloning centers / Revolution

3SG1: I was thinking that they must be scared that your letter is spreading and they are now exposed. But I am at the point where I am tired of motherf******s thinking just because they have power, money and their technologies, I fear them?! That's never the case. I'm David and they are Goliath. No oddball scares me. They don't scare me, they p*** me off! I also think they are cowards; hiding and f****** with kids. Pop in my hood and do that bull-s*** and watch what will happen to your throne sitting a**. Donald, please let the revolution begin so I can go HAM [Hard As a Motherf****r] and let loose on these motherf*****s... damn. I'm tired of reading and waiting for the truth to [fully] come out and waiting for the revolution to start...

DM: Half of the people who attend the cloning center(s) _as REM driven clone duplicates of themselves (through the process of consciousness transfer from their original bodies to their REM driven clones located at the cloning center)_ AT the cloning center(s) want the cloning center(s) shut down. Half of the people who are activated as _REM driven_ clone versions of themselves at the cloning center do not want to be activated as _REM driven_ clones or cloned anymore. The shutdown of the cloning centers all hinges on Queen Elizabeth II and other Royal families and the power (Illuminati) families who attend the cloning centers _as REM driven copies of their original selves._ You have no idea how heavy the tension is _at the cloning centers_ right now... Many people _who are activated as their REM driven clone versions_ at the cloning centers are all freaking out, trying to jump ship. People who work for Facebook and also attend the cloning center _as REM driven clones_, say that: "Posting about the Illuminati, REM driven cloning, and disclosing all that the Illuminati do is freedom of speech." Also none of the power elite families, royals, and other loyal Illuminati members and Illuminati factions who attend the cloning centers _as REM driven clone versions of themselves_ want ME to have my day in court; whether it is for slandering names, or inciting a panic, none of the power elite families, royals, and other loyal Illuminati members and Illuminati factions for which the shutdown of the cloning centers hinges on want me to go to court –none of them want ME to go to court. I will spill the beans about EVERYTHING in an intelligible polite manner, all for permanent public record. _As REM driven clones at the cloning center_, the power elite families, royals, and other loyal Illuminati members and Illuminati factions were discussing the possibility about shutting down Facebook with a "hacker" but then opted to do nothing... However the Illuminati members punished my _REM driven_ clones badly when I was activated as a _REM driven_ clone at the cloning center _(through the process of consciousness transfer from my original body to my REM driven clone located at the cloning center)._ The last three days when I was _activated as a REM driven clone_ at the cloning center, the only thing the Illuminati members _(also REM driven clone versions of original people)_ did was talk to me _(as REM driven clones at the cloning center)._ However, last night, the Illuminati punished my _REM driven_ clones badly; a few celebrities harmed my _REM driven_ clones, including Queen Elizabeth II _(as a REM driven clone of herself, harmed my REM driven clone)_; as well as, Phil Reece. Phil Reece is a Commissionaire (doorman in uniform) for the Canadian Security Intelligence Service (C.S.I.S). Phil Reece _as a REM driven clone of himself_, smashed me when I was _activated as a REM driven clone_ at the cloning center. Phil Reece _(as a REM driven clone of himself)_ got a bat and smashed my _REM driven_ clone to a pulp at the cloning center. I'll tell you about the experience later in a new update. **April 25, 2012 at 4:21pm**

Deaths

Robert Pickton Murders

DM: Queen Elizabeth II had a role to play in the Robert Pickton murders. Just the Pickton murders alone should get Queen Elizabeth II (the original, and NOT ANY of her clones) hanged. Queen Elizabeth II, *as a REM driven clone of herself at the cloning station*, as well as, other Illuminati members *(as REM driven clone versions)*, made me watch the footage of the Pickton murders *when I was a REM driven clone version of myself* at the cloning centers. The footage was terrible. Robert Pickton was smashing prostitutes with a ball-peen hammer from behind... I saw all / most of the murders *as a REM driven clone* at the cloning center... The Illuminati taped all the Pickton murders and watch it at the cloning center, as *REM driven* clone versions of original people. The Illuminati are very sick people and are desensitised to human suffering. I have to tell the world about all of this, if not for myself then for all the others trapped at the cloning centers *(as REM driven clones, as well as, real people in their original bodies)* too, who are too scared to talk for fear of death at the hands of the Illuminati... **April 14, 2012 at 6:09pm**

DM: Robert Pickton, the pig farmer, killed approximately 40 prostitutes near Toronto and once the prostitutes were dead he fed the bodies to the pigs on his farm. However, what people are unaware of is that the Canadian government were also complicit in the Robert Pickton murders. The Canadian government were trying to figure out a way to get more prostitutes off the streets of Toronto. I guess there were prostitutes all over the region of Toronto, and as a result: the Canadian government put Robert Pickton to the task of reducing the population of prostitutes. The accomplices in the Robert Pickton murders deliberately placed a camera positioned in the corner of Robert Pickton's "killing room". Robert Pickton would later bring these women to his home and lead them to the "killing room" where he would show each woman a painting on the wall... As Robert Pickton and each woman visiting his home stood side by side, admiring the painting on his wall, he would reach into the back pocket for the ball-peen hammer and then he would smash each woman in the back of the head with the ball-peen hammer. Robert Pickton killed each one of his victims by smashing the women in the back of the head with a ball-peen hammer, approximately 38-40 women. All these murders are on video for Prime Minster Stephen Harper and his cronies to watch at the cloning center *(as REM driven clone versions of themselves)*. Prime Minster Stephen Harper and his Illuminati cronies *(as REM driven clones)*, laugh and cheer when the women died... many, many people have watched these Robert Pickton murders *(as REM driven clones)* at the cloning center... Moreover, the RCMP (Royal Canadian Mounted Police) destroyed the Robert Pickton house (where the murders took place) when Robert Pickton was eventually stopped. The RCMP did not look for evidence for too long and covered up the crimes... The Illuminati made me watch all of the murders of these women *as a REM driven clone version of myself* at the cloning centers... I want to bring the Illuminati members who had a role to play in the Robert Pickton murders to justice... I want revenge upon them... **April 14, 2012 at 6:20pm**

3SG1: No, [the Robert Pickton murders] that was in Abbotsford near Vancouver.

DM: The Illuminati members said that the prostitutes were from Toronto. Well the main point is that prostitutes were murdered and I was forced to watch the murders on video *as a REM driven clone at the cloning center*... it was gruesome! **April 14, 2012 at 6:22pm**

3SG2: Prostitutes do not pay taxes to Prime Minster Stephen Harper/Queen Elizabeth II/The Pope. That is why they don't like them. The Pope is the biggest pimp of all.

DM: Queen Elizabeth II hates prostitutes... I do not know the reason why... It is ironic because she is more piggish and vulgar than any prostitute on the planet. Seriously, you should see what Queen Elizabeth II does *as a REM driven clone* in the privacy of the cloning center... hairy tits to the breeze, no shame, no class. Queen Elizabeth II is a piggish hag, grotesque and vulgar. **April 14, 2012 at 6:26pm**

Donald Marshall's Health

General Health

3SG1: I hope you are OK.

DM: No. I'm not OK. I am feeling unhealthier in a weird way with every passing day due to *REM driven* cloning torture which affects me in my original body because consciousness is linked. **April 22, 2012 at 6:08pm** ·

3SG1: Hey Donny, hope you are feeling better.... oh yeah light it, don't fight it! Stay strong bro.

3SG2: We're always here for you dude, no worry, got you covered!

DM: I think of you guys when I am *a REM driven clone version of myself*, barefoot in the dirt arena of the cloning center; then I start to think of *(the original and real)* Queen Elizabeth II (and NOT her clone) in a courtroom, shaking... *As a REM driven clone of myself at the cloning center*, I laugh at the Illuminati *REM driven clones* and call them "Pathetic heathen filth"... and laugh... the Illuminati *REM driven clones* are just going to hurt me *as a REM driven clone of myself at the cloning center*, somehow anyway, so there is no point in being civil.... is there? **May 15, 2012 at 6:20pm** ·

3SG2: [There is no point in being civil, just] be yourself!

Microchips in Donald Marshall's original (real) body

3SG1: Have the Illuminati come for the real you and taken your real body to that center? Have you been programmed, like is there a microchip in your body?

DM: I know there is a microchip in me somewhere, and it is a Global Positioning System (GPS) microchip. I do not even know where *in my original body* it is. **April 22, 2012 at 7:27pm**

Mistaken Identity: The "Donald Marshall" exposing the Illuminati still lives

3SG1: I heard Donald Marshall is dead?

3SG2: It's not the same Donald Marshall.

DM: No I am not dead, that is a different guy; he is Native Indian. I am white, and I am still alive... for now... my heart hurts badly though. The Illuminati _REM driven clones_ got me badly last time I was unwillingly activated as a _REM driven_ clone at the cloning center. I am very sick _in my original body_ from _REM driven_ clone torture. I did not want to visit the library to use their computers today, but I have to. Mailing and posting about the Illuminati and their REM driven cloning subculture is my only hope to escape the cloning centers, and being activated as _REM driven_ clone at the cloning center. **April 26, 2012 at 7:11pm ·**

Donald Marshall's Mission

Donald Marshall's life purpose

3SG1: I am so sorry Donald!!

DM: Me too... but the Illuminati will be stopped. My life's purpose is to destroy them now. Help me spread the truth about them [regarding REM driven cloning, as well as, all that I have disclosed]... Spreading the truth about the Illuminati's REM driven subculture and their evil deeds against humanity is working. People are freaking out and demanding answers. When a large group demand lie detector (independent ones) tests of individuals involved with REM driven cloning, who are not memory suppressed and remember fully once they wake up, this will be a downhill battle and the cloning centers, as well as the Illuminati will be shut down. **March 28, 2012 at 10:52pm**

Read / Print / Share information regarding the Illuminati's REM driven subculture

3SG1: Donald, do you want this information [regarding your whistle blowing disclosures] public?

DM: Yes I want it public but wait, other organizations are coordinating with each other to bring it out all at once, tell your family and friends for now; soon blitzkrieg. **March 28, 2012 at 10:59pm**

Why it makes little difference if Donald Marshall travels to a different country

3SG1: Donald why don't you come to China where we can protect you? We cannot protect you if you are not careful, and we cannot pull this through if you are dead... I have been losing patience since the first time I heard about this. I still recommend you go to China...

DM: The Illuminati always know where I am [through the GPS tracking microchip which they imbedded in me, the RFID the implants, and through the camera they installed under the optical nerve in my right eye]. The Illuminati can kill me anytime they want on a whim by torturing my _REM driven_ clone really badly and constantly at the cloning center... This will cause me to die of a heart attack or aneurysm _in my original body_ because consciousness is linked. The Illuminati do NOT want me dead.

DM: They want to torture me for sport and as an evil spectacle for celebrities. They also want me to make the odd song for Rihanna or Justin Timberlake; or Selena Gomez or Justin Bieber who all attend the cloning center [as REM driven clones of themselves when they go to sleep] and got 95% of the songs they have sang from me. I have to escape the cloning centers. They still transfer my consciousness *to my REM driven clone* when I sleep and bring me there; then they beg me: "Are you sure you don't want to hang with us?" "Can't you please just stay with us? Join us? We love you." "No? Well then, we are going to torture you! [as a REM driven clone]" It is so old and overdone. Queen Elizabeth II [as a REM driven clone version of herself] cackling and making threats... then saying "She loves me. I'm amazing." Then she asks: "Will I join them?" I say "No!" Then Queen Elizabeth II's [as a REM driven clone] face scrunches up, the insults start once more, and Queen Elizabeth II or someone else at the cloning center croaks a death threat at me... and it goes on monotonously like that... rinse and repeat. Queen Elizabeth II is a retarded woman [as a REM driven clone, at the cloning center]. **April 3, 2012 at 8:44pm**

Donald Marshall on: the Illuminati REM driven clones and other public figures

3SG1: Donald, I didn't even know who Tila Tequila was. I just stumbled on Tila Tequila, through randomly browsing YouTube and it was quite the story. I couldn't believe what I was reading but then you (Donald Marshall) came onto the scene with an amazing story I was definitely curious.

DM: I hate Tila Tequila. I hate them all. I will crush Queen Elizabeth II's cloning paedophile stations and her empire with what I know, but I need the help of others. Help me spread the letter (Donald Marshall Proboards 2012), the Full Disclosure (Marshall 2015b), Summary Disclosure (Marshall 2015a), as well as, all the disclosures documents concerning the Illuminati's REM driven cloning subculture. **April 18, 2012 at 6:29pm**

DM: OH BY THE WAY: look at my pictures on Facebook here, and compare these photos to the Megadeth album cover (2001) I use as a profile picture. <u>**April 18, 2012 at 6:29pm**</u>

3SG1: I did check out your photos in comparison to the Megadeth album cover (2001) and I can definitely see the resemblance. Wow. So now there is a tonne of stuff I want to know but do not even know where to start...

Facebook Post: Comparing Donald Marshall's pictures with the Megadeth album cover

DM: ATTENTION: MY FRIENDS: Look at my pictures which I took with the BlackBerry and compare the pictures I have taken, with the Megadeth album cover (2001), I use as a Facebook profile picture. Click on my pictures again to enlarge the pictures. Tell me what you think. The Megadeth album is called "The World Needs A Hero" (2001)... how appropriate a title. Look, look, my pictures are "public" [on Facebook], look.

Donald Marshall on: How to comprehend the subject of REM driven cloning

3SG1: For someone who is supposed to be suffering from the most horrendous and bizarre torture and trying to expose the biggest, most powerful and vile Mafioso criminal ring of paedophiles and sadists, you sure sound trite and petty with your continuous "Look at me. Look at me." Are you sure you are not just an attention seeker, trying to get attention by getting loads of people to feel sorry for you? I bet you are even taking donations from people.

DM: Wow! What a comment to make! All it is, is highly advanced science and technology hidden and in secret. That's it. It is science and technology the general public is currently unaware of and it currently exists and it is real. You really shouldn't make harsh and unwarranted comments when it comes to a subject matter you have little understanding of: REM driven cloning. You'll end up looking really stupid when this is all proven clearly. REM driven cloning / human cloning is referenced all throughout life covertly: in movies, music, art, literature etc. Moreover, references to REM driven cloning / human cloning exists EVERYWHERE and exists around everyone's presence at all times currently in life. However, nobody in current history has told the public about the Illuminati's REM driven cloning subculture plainly, but it does exist and it is referenced all throughout life. REM driven cloning / human cloning references life, and life references REM driven cloning / human cloning: such corroborations does not happen when someone is lying. Do not be so quick to jump to conclusions and berate me; it will hinder your ability to learn something new which is directly in front of your eyes –except nobody has ever directed the publics' attention to REM driven cloning. REM driven cloning / human cloning is real and it exists. And no I haven't asked for donations or received any. A couple of people offered to buy me a computer so that I could mail around the clock. You always have something negative to say, as if you work for the Illuminati or something. If you do not want to read it, block me. Otherwise keep quiet, and do not inhibit your ability to learn something new which becomes blatantly obvious once a person reaches a stage where all the circumstantial evidence and corroborative evidence I will present demonstrates that REM driven cloning is real and a fact of life. I am only presenting facts of life; I am not speculating or guessing. These are firsthand eyewitness accounts presented freely to the public, for the express purpose for the public to help end this Mafioso criminal ring of paedophiles and sadists. This is too important for me to debate... trite and petty? Look at me, look at me? I did not even want my face to be shown (on Facebook)... but I have to... If you are not interested in REM driven human cloning why don't you go and find something else to do? **April 19, 2012 at 2:15pm**

DM: I cannot really blame her though. It is hard to believe anyone would be as scummy as the Illuminati, but the Illuminati are that scummy. **April 21, 2012 at 7:39pm**

3SG2: That does look like you on the cover of the album.

DM: Yes. It is not enough though. I need the polygraph tests done. The accuracy of polygraph tests have improved now in the last five years. Polygraph tests have improved their accuracy rating from 75% to approximately 90% accuracy. Some people have looked at the pictures of me on Facebook, and compared it to the image on the cover of the Megadeth Album cover *The World Needs A Hero* (2001) and had an anxiety attack. There are so many people writing to me now. I do not have enough online time to respond to them all. I try though. It is a good thing I type fast. **April 21, 2012 at 7:47pm**

Why Donald Marshall CANNOT pass off his firsthand eyewitness accounts as "Fiction"

3SG1: Donald, you ought to be contacting a publisher; an independent publisher of course and not a big mainstream company to get your letters published. It will most likely be written off as "Fiction" but having your letters published will get a lot of readers, especially in conspiracy magazines too. This could be a way to address that particular audience.

DM: I cannot pass off these firsthand eyewitness accounts as fiction when they are **not**. They are real and happen as a result of highly advanced science and technology *(hidden and in secret): through the process of consciousness transfer from my original body to a REM driven clone when I reach REM sleep (in my original body at home) to a remote location in an above ground cloning center in Canada.*

Too many lives depend on this information reaching many people and therefore it cannot be passed off as fiction. It is real and the world must know. Moreover, I cannot mention peoples' names in something like that (in a work of fiction); they will charge me with slander and copyright infringement of their names if they are famous. I have to tell as many people as possible the reality of the situation... the more eyes and ears, the better at this stage. Once I tell people what really happened with 9/11 and the pentagon "plane" that wasn't even a plane, THEN the *REM driven clones of* Illuminati members are going to tear my *REM driven* clone(s) apart whenever I reach REM sleep and I am activated as a *REM driven* clone at the cloning center. Furthermore, when I make Document2 the *REM driven* clones of loyal Illuminati members at the cloning center said that every name I mention is going to take turns turning me inside out or whatever they want to do to my *REM driven* clone, one by one, while all the other *REM driven* clones sitting in the stands watch. Such torture carried out on my *REM driven* clones, one by one, from each name that I mention in Document2 will mostly likely give me a heart attack *in my original body* (because consciousness is linked; Petkova and Ehrsson 2008; Ehrsson 2013). I think I may almost have a heart attack or an aneurysm right now.

DM: Therefore I must have a large audience read all this information, all at once and act immediately, if you can understand my dilemma? Moreover, with the limited amount of time I have online each day, where I am answering questions on Facebook and in Hotmail, and messaging others constantly and posting the letter wherever I can; I am pretty desperate to get this information out to a large audience as soon as possible and you would be too, if you were in my situation *and your consciousness was being transferred from your original body to your REM driven clone duplicate at an undisclosed location far away from your home while you slept, each time you entered REM sleep (90-110 minutes after first falling asleep)*, trust me. The torture of *REM driven* clones hurts just as badly as if the attacks were being carried out on your original (real) body. This is because consciousness is flexible, as well as linked (Petkova and Ehrsson 2008; Ehrsson 2013). Furthermore, because the Illuminati can control the pain sensors of REM clones at the cloning center, by remote control with the push of a button, they can turn up the pain threshold for what is "normal" for a human being. Therefore, the Illuminati can make a person who has had their consciousness transferred to their *REM driven* clone feel pain beyond what they would normally feel in their original body. I must get out of the cloning centers permanently, and help others who are also trapped there *(as REM driven clones, and in their original bodies)* get out too; others who are either too scared to talk for fear of death and torture *(as REM driven clones, or in their original body)*; or others who do not want to betray their parents who are Illuminati members who attend the cloning centers willingly. Sometimes entire families attend the cloning centers *as REM driven duplicate clones of themselves*. Help me spread the truth guys. You know more places than I do. **April 19, 2012 at 8:00pm**

Donald Marshall on: "Zeitgeist" and the activist Michael Moore

3SG1: Well those of us who question everything already know about 9/11 false flag attack. You just have to watch "Zeitgeist" and the truth about all our wars and the misinformation planned catalysts that gave them the ability to make us believe we needed to fight and go to war. Simple examples include: sinking of Lusitania; Pearl harbour; Gulf of Tonkin incident, first bombing of World Trade Center (epic fail) and 9/11, and now it looks like they are going to sink the enterprise of the oldest most ill equipped aircraft carrier. We have, and it is headed for the Strait of Hormuz. It has eight nuclear reactors and is scheduled to be decommissioned yet it is being sent into the 'lion's den'; then they are going to sink it and blame it on Iran and that is why we have to attack Iran next... It is just more misinformation but business as usual and the sheeple of this country will say "Support the troops man, they fight for our freedom!" Only as usual our brave brothers and sisters will be risking their lives to further the elites plan not to guarantee our freedoms, as the puppet masters want you to believe... we all know what is going on here, some of us more than others... but everyday more of the end-game becomes obvious. Our new slogan for this country should be "FREEDOM ISN'T FREE, IT COSTS YOU YOUR FREEDOMS" and if you have oil or resources, yes we are taking them too, to join our New World Order, or we will invent stories, lie, invade and take your country for everything it is worth, while at the same time making much money selling supplies for war.

DM: Well said and true mostly. However the Zeitgeist movie is made BY the Illuminati. "Zeitgeist" is what the Germans (German faction of the Illuminati) call me at the cloning center as REM driven clones. It means "Century Ghost" or "Spirit of the Century". The Zeitgeist movement, is that the one the activist Michael Moore is part of? Michael Moore is always looking for "justice", and that in itself is funny! Michael Moore is IN the Illuminati, and attends the cloning center _as a REM driven clone_. Michael Moore knows the truth about 9/11, REM driven cloning / the cloning centers, and Michael Moore knows who I am... and Michael Moore is out talking to people on TV acting as if he is on their side, funny stuff... However the Illuminati made that online Zeitgeist movie; only the thermite cut I-beams are computer generated. The Illuminati also make fake alien sightings to throw people off the real scent, which is: cloning / REM driven cloning. It is **ALL** about cloning / REM driven cloning. The Illuminati ONLY discuss the most important and biggest things _as REM driven clones_ at the cloning center, and **ONLY** at the cloning center. They do NOT discuss anything important in the Freemason Lodge; it is only minor talk at the Freemason Lodge. The cloning centers are where Illuminati members meet _as REM driven clones_ and the cloning centers are such secret meeting places that there are no bugs there; no eavesdropping etc. The Illuminati members have discussed their shadier dealings right in front of me, _as REM driven clone versions of ourselves at the cloning center_ as an attempt to try to impress me with their power and as a boast of TOTAL confidence that the Illuminati members will never be caught and no one will EVER know... People know now though... Keep spreading the word guys... my life depends on it seriously. **April 19, 2012 at 8:29pm**

Suggested alternative approaches to exposing the Illuminati's REM driven subculture

3SG1: Do you have a webcam or microphone? You can create songs that talk about what you went through, and upload them onto YouTube, and in that way, you can get your message out to more people. Very few people are willing to read a long letter, but a lot more are likely to get the message from a song.

DM: Hmm. That IS a possibility... however mailing the letter is working though. The Illuminati members *as REM driven clones of themselves*, talked with me *(also a REM driven clone of myself)* for the past three days at the cloning center. The Illuminati members talked, and begged, and talked *(as REM driven clone versions of ourselves at the cloning center)*. As *REM driven clones of themselves at the cloning center*, the Illuminati members wanted me to stop mailing the letter *(when I wake up and I am no longer a REM driven clone –because the original person's consciousness overrides the REM driven clone's consciousness)* and I said back to them *(as a REM driven clone of me at the cloning center)* "Stop bringing me here then you miserable wretched pig faced hag". The Illuminati have been tracking the spread of the letter as best as they can, and I guess many, many people have read it, and spread it... and the Illuminati are worried... **April 23, 2012 at 4:02pm**

Full exposure of REM driven cloning is the Illuminati's GREATEST FEAR

DM: Actually I will get more in depth on the matter later, but the Illuminati fear **three** things really:

1) Muslims (suicide bombers) -can't do much about them;

2) Nuclear war (can't really do much about that), and;

3) The populace finding out about human cloning, REM driven (human) cloning / the cloning centers.

Their fear is because people would rise up in numbers and protest and demand answers IF a large amount of people found out about REM driven cloning and realise it is a fact of life which has been used as a method to commit crimes against the populace undetected (while the populace slept). That is the stage we are in now: informing as many people as possible about the reality of REM driven cloning, and how the Illuminati really communicate with each other in secret: through the process of consciousness transfer to their REM driven clones when they sleep *(and reach REM sleep, 90-110 minutes after falling first falling asleep)*. Spreading the letter and informing as many people as possible about the reality of REM driven cloning MUST be working because the Illuminati ARE worried.

Inform the world about the Illuminati's REM driven human cloning subculture RAPIDLY

DM: *As REM driven clone versions of ourselves at the cloning center*, the Illuminati members are NOW asking me to stop mailing the letter, instead of torturing my *REM driven* clones at the cloning center. The Illuminati members told me *(when I was a REM driven clone at the cloning center through the process of consciousness transfer from my original body when I am in REM sleep to my REM driven clone)* they didn't want to have to kill me *(the real me / my original body)* as I have done so much for the Illuminati *as a REM driven clone at the cloning center*, and the Illuminati members think I am something special. However, the Illuminati members *(as REM driven clones of themselves at the cloning center)* said they eventually will kill me if I do not stop mailing the letter, and then people will hear that I died of a heart attack or aneurysm *in my original body (which happens as a result of the constant torture of REM driven clones, because consciousness is linked. Therefore constant torture of a person's REM driven clones will cause the person to die of a heart attack or aneurysm in their original body)* and they will say "Oh my God!" —and spread the letter more frantically, but the spreading of the letter will eventually settle down after a while; this is when Queen Elizabeth II will resume cloning the populaces' children and suck on the children *as REM driven clones at the cloning center*. Basically, that is what Queen Elizabeth II does to the children who are brought to the cloning centers *as REM driven clones (through the process of consciousness transfer, from their original bodies to their REM driven duplicate clones)*.

Queen Elizabeth II's crimes against the children of the world as REM driven clones

DM: I am sorry if it sounds gross but that is generally what the hag (Queen Elizabeth II) does *as a REM driven clone version of herself at the cloning center*. Queen Elizabeth II *as a REM driven clone at the cloning center*, sometimes also tortures the *REM driven* clones of random children who are unsuspectingly brought to the cloning centers *(through the process of consciousness transfer from the children's original bodies to their REM driven clone bodies —when they reach REM sleep (at home in bed) —usually 90-110 minutes after first falling asleep)* while other *REM driven* clones sitting in the stands of the arena watch. It is very surreal. There are hundreds of *REM driven* clones, all just sitting there while Queen Elizabeth II *as a REM driven clone at the cloning center* commits her heinous crimes. Some of the *REM driven* clones sitting in the stands, look at their feet, other *REM driven* clones sitting in the stands cry (as Queen Elizabeth II *as a REM driven clone of herself* commits her crimes in front of on looking *REM driven* clones sitting in the stands at the cloning center). I MUST tell the world about REM driven cloning... The populace MUST shut down the cloning centers.

The Illuminati are not embarrassed to commit their crimes as REM driven clones

DM: The cloning centers are worse than one can imagine. You would think these people in the public eye would be embarrassed to do such things in front of everyone, or you would think they would be embarrassed to commit these crimes in front of everyone (even if they are _REM driven_ clones of their original versions –you would think they would be embarrassed) but they are not. I do not understand their lack of feeling shame either. It is an invented paedophile religion –this REM driven cloning subculture. Paedophilia is the BASIS for the Illuminati's REM driven cloning religion, as well as "pain". I have no choice but to tell everyone about REM driven cloning and the monstrous crimes committed against humanity unsuspectingly (while the populace sleeps). The Illuminati are still transferring my consciousness against my will to my _REM driven_ clone duplicate when I reach REM sleep _(in my original body)_ and activating me as a _REM driven_ clone at the cloning center _(located within a 5/6 hour drive of the Robert Pickton Farm in Canada)_. **April 23, 2012 at 4:21pm**

Why Donald Marshall is still alive

3SG1: Donald, if you are telling the truth, the Illuminati would have killed you, why haven't they killed you?

DM: Yes the Illuminati would kill me but I have made so many songs _as a REM driven clone version of me at the cloning center_; toy ideas, cartoon ideas, movie ideas, and even clothes – all of which I did as a _REM driven_ clone at the cloning center through the process of consciousness transfer from my original body to my duplicate REM driven clone (when I reach REM sleep). I have mostly made songs as a _REM driven_ clone at the cloning center though, and the Illuminati told me _as REM driven clone versions of ourselves_: "If there is anyone on earth they would give pause to before executing it is me"; and I believe them. I did many things as a _REM driven_ clone at the cloning center.

The Illuminati want me to continue to make songs for them _as a REM driven clone version of me at the cloning center_ and just hang out at the cloning centers with the Illuminati; help the Illuminati with movies; movie lines and other such nonsense. **April 24, 2012 at 7:59pm**

Donald Marshall on: how he aims to fully expose REM driven cloning

3SG1: Donald, I appreciate what you are doing. You need to have people corroborate this; people who have also been to the cloning centers and remember in real life. You have to get the lie detector tests done, so that this is proven once and for all, and you have to get others to take lie detector tests too. If what you are saying is true then the CIA must be tracking you, and I can understand that you are not bragging, you are just informing the world about this dire situation, and you must mention how you came about acquiring such knowledge. You must be scared at the same time, but you have to think of a better way to stop them, think of better way to prove cloning to the average person. Tell us the locations of the cloning centers, show us detailed maps etc. so people can verify this once and for all and we can bring a stop to them!

DM: Wow that was passionate. Well... all I can do is have my nephew who has also been a _REM driven_ clone at the cloning centers verify this by detailing his experiences and what he has seen as at the cloning centers _through the process of consciousness transfer from his original body to his REM driven clone._ He wants to help and does not want me to be activated as _REM driven_ clones at the cloning center anymore. My nephew has not been a _REM driven_ clone at the cloning center for many years since he freaked out _as a REM driven clone_ at the cloning center. Moreover, independent polygraph tests would remove any shadow of doubt, and I am also constructing a list of names of everyone I have seen as a _REM driven_ clone at the cloning center, and what each person as their _REM driven_ clone duplicate, at the cloning center has done to other _REM driven_ clones and real people _(in their original bodies)_, as well as, what I know firsthand that each person I name has done in real life.

The CIA is tracking everything Donald Marshall does from the cloning center

DM: Yes, the CIA track everything at the cloning center and the CIA interrogate me _(as a REM driven clone at the cloning center)_ about the (Facebook) posts and punish me as a _REM driven clone_ at the cloning center for writing (and exposing REM driven cloning and the Illuminati) but I have no choice. The colossal amount of songs, toy ideas, movie ideas, cartoon concepts and stuff are **NOT** the issue, and YOU ARE right. I am **not** bragging; look back in my posts, I never have. I'm just raising awareness about this (REM driven cloning) and I was waiting for a larger audience or venue before I released Document2 (list of names of everyone I remember seeing as REM driven clones at the cloning center) because the Illuminati warned me that when I finish Document2 _(list of names who attend the cloning centers as REM driven clone copies of their original selves)_ and try and send Document2 around I would be grilled at the cloning center _as a REM driven clone_ badly; by everyone I mention who attends the cloning center _as a REM driven clone of themselves_, one by one assembly line style, and I might have a heart attack or aneurysm / stroke in my original body, due to the constant torture of my _REM driven_ clones _(because consciousness is linked, and constant torture of a person's REM driven clone causes the person to have a heart attack or aneurysm in their original body –while they sleep)._

Why Donald Marshall continues to inform the world about REM driven cloning

DM: My heart is messed up now from the intermittent *REM driven* clone torture I suffer at the cloning centers, and yes, I am very scared. I am a 36 year old man without money and connections; against the richest and most powerful people in the world, but I have no choice, I have to mail... it's the only way to stop the Illuminati and their REM driven cloning subculture and shut down the cloning centers. The populace demanding answers about REM driven cloning, human cloning and the cloning centers is the only way to stop the Illuminati and shut down the cloning centers. You would be mailing the world and informing the world about REM driven cloning and the Illuminati if you were in my situation but you MUST understand the Illuminati cover their tracks incredibly well... they were never going to tell me the location of the cloning center(s) when the Illuminati transfer my consciousness and activate me as a *REM driven* clone while I sleep (at home in bed).

What Donald Marshall knows about the location of the cloning center

DM: Willing Illuminati members do not even know the location of the cloning centers, and they are loyal to the Illuminati. These willing Illuminati members just get "cloned in". However, I have seen the outside of the cloning center *as a REM driven clone*, it has grass all around the small sports venue looking place; there isn't a parking lot, there aren't roads; and roughly 100 yards from the small sports venue looking place, there are trees as far as the eye can see. There are no signs of civilisation but the place behind you, I call it "The Diddle Dome" (the cloning center). The Illuminati hate it when I call the cloning centers "The Diddle Dome".

The Illuminati does NOT have a contingency plan. SPREAD the truth about REM cloning

DM: When the world starts asking questions about REM driven cloning and the cloning centers, the Illuminati plan to have every celebrity / public figure known, to start making skits and parody songs about 'Donald Marshall and the cloning center situation', to make those who are still unaware of the reality of the situation laugh, and to make those who are still uniformed regarding REM driven cloning and the cloning centers disregard the truth. The Illuminati do not have a contingency plan. The Illuminati just hopes that no one starts asking questions about REM driven cloning and the cloning centers. Help me spread the truth about what the Illuminati do (REM driven cloning) and what they do every day (REM driven cloning)! Spreading the truth about REM driven cloning and the cloning centers is the only way to stop the Illuminati. **April 26, 2012 at 7:09pm**

Document 2

Document 2: A List of people who have attended the cloning centers as REM driven clones.

3SG1: Make that list [of people who have attended the cloning centers as REM driven clones] SOON. I will spread it. I am a beast when it comes to researching and exposing so count on me!

DM: I love people like you... you are smart enough to recognize the ring of truth... I will make the list but it will take some time because it is LONG. The list will include the biggest stars in Hollywood; musicians: only the biggest musicians; and most of the world leaders, (except for a few world leaders), and an incredible collection of extremely rich Jewish people –who all attend the cloning centers *as REM driven clone versions of themselves when they go to sleep (through the process of consciousness transfer to the REM driven clone)*. It is going to be a long list. Also there is something BIG that I must disclose which is very bad and I haven't mentioned yet... It will shake the world, but I am waiting for the world's eye before I make this disclosure... I need world attention now... I am getting very sick from the torture of my *REM driven* clones and I am getting sick of the Illuminati. I am very sick from it all. I need an old computer or a laptop so that I can mail from home around the clock, instead of 2 hours a day at the library... some days I am too sick (from the torture of my *REM driven* clones) to go to the library and mail. **April 12, 2012 at 6:59pm**

The progress of Document2

3SG1: What's up? How's part 2 coming?

DM: With two hours online on average a day, where I have been responding to messages regarding REM driven cloning and the Illuminati and when I am still posting updates about my experiences from the cloning center *as a REM driven clone*, and mailing the letter as far and wide as I can, I do not have enough time to respond to all the messages I receive. I am very popular all the sudden. Therefore, constructing Document2 will take approximately two days where I will need to concentrate fully on Document2 and I will not be able to respond to messages, detail my *REM driven* cloning experiences or post the letter on various websites. The Illuminati are going to punish me badly when I go to sleep and they transfer my consciousness *from my original body* to my *REM driven* clone, after I release the list of names of everyone I have seen at the cloning center *as a REM driven clone*, and what these people have done to other people, at the cloning center and in real life. Therefore, I want the largest audience I can get when I release Document2... mass mail Document2 and send. **April 21, 2012 at 7:07pm**

Donald Marshall and his friends thoughts on Document2

3SG1: Eagerly waiting for part 2 [Document2].

DM: Document2 will be released as soon as I have enough eyes looking at Document1 (The Letter about the Illuminati's REM driven cloning subculture (Donald Marshall Proboards 2012)). I cannot afford to have this blow over and fizzle out... If I fail, I am doomed. **May 4, 2012 at 6:13pm**

3SG2: Good [that Document 2 will be released soon]! Donald, I am glad I caught you! We really think you are great! Have a good day. I hope everything is turning around.

DM: Thank you 3SG2. Keep showing everyone the letter; we have the Illuminati on the ropes now. **May 4, 2012 at 6:24pm** ·

3SG2: Donald, if you can give me another write up, I will post your accounts of REM driven cloning again on the American Patriots Friends Network (A.P.F.N) and we have MANY READERS! I am so HAPPY for you... take care.

DM: That is awesome! Many people started emailing me after the A.P.F.N post you made 3SG2. Thank you. Keep up the good work guys. You are saving me from REM driven cloning and crushing the Illuminati and their REM driven cloning subculture with every post of that letter. **May 4, 2012 at 7:24pm**

3SG2: You made my day, Donald! I have reposted your first letter (Donald Marshall Proboards 2012) to the public!

DM: Cool. With any luck the Illuminati will not activate me as a REM driven clone at the cloning center and the Illuminati will attempt to lay low. The Illuminati are worried now. Too many people are learning about their REM driven cloning subculture and sending the information about the Illuminati's REM driven cloning subculture to all the right places. I WILL escape the Illuminati and their REM driven cloning subculture and I WILL shut down the Illuminati and I WILL shut down the cloning centers. I can't wait... **May 4, 2012 at 7:36pm**

Tracking

3SG1: Donald, are you being tracked?

DM: I am being tracked certainly. For example there is Global Positioning System (GPS) located in my original body somewhere, somehow. Moreover, every Facebook post I make is known by the Illuminati, everything I do. The Illuminati members have interrogated me *as a REM driven clone* at the cloning center and tortured my *REM driven* clones regarding what I have said and posted on Facebook and elsewhere. The Illuminati *members as REM driven clone versions of themselves at the cloning center* would have tortured my *REM driven* clone(s) anyway with some made-up excuse to torture me *as a REM driven clone* even if I was not posting about what the Illuminati do and disclosing all Illuminati secrets; so I have no choice and I have nothing to lose... um, help me world. REM driven cloning and all I have disclosed about the Illuminati is true and there is much more to disclose. **April 29, 2012 at 7:32pm**

People helping Donald Marshall

3SG1: On a different website I posted your letter (Donald Marshall Proboards 2012) and within a day and a half it was viewed by over one hundred people.

DM: That is awesome. Keep spreading the letter (Donald Marshall Proboards 2012) to the world my friends; this is working... **May 8, 2012 at 6:32pm** ·

May 14th 2012

3SG1 posts a warning to "The Evil Ones" on Donald Marshall's Facebook timeline

3SG1: TO THE EVIL ONES: BE AWARE THAT IF DONALD DIES WE RELENTLESSLY ACCELERATE OUR EXPOSURE OF YOU A HUNDRED THOUSAND-FOLD. NO STONE WILL BE UNTURNED!

DM: Thank you so much. The Illuminati members know this. I think it is thanks to the help of so many people like you which may be half the reason I am still alive. The Illuminati members will see this post *as REM driven clone versions of themselves* at the cloning center and they will question me about this post when I am activated as a *REM driven* clone at the cloning center. The Illuminati *REM driven clones* will either talk to me about this post *as REM driven clone versions of ourselves at the cloning center* or attack me when I am activated as a *REM driven* clone at the cloning center. I really hope the Illuminati members never activate me as a *REM driven* clone ever again! I will be going home soon. I will give an update tomorrow on my status and what happens at the cloning center if the Illuminati members decide to activate me as a *REM driven* clone when I go to sleep this evening. Hopefully nothing happens... The Illuminati members are so arrogant OR, they were so arrogant and something changed... They must know they are as good as caught now... I have been wondering what tipped the scales and now I know... It is all of you... Thank you all... I will post and message many things tomorrow... **May 15, 2012 at 2:02am**

Research "Monarch slaves" and "Monarch survivors" to grasp Donald Marshall's plight

3SG2: Donald, you have not said anything new in your letter (Donald Marshall Proboards 2012) that I did not know before. There are many videos available on YouTube discussing what you disclosed in your letter. Research "Monarch slaves" or "Monarch Survivors"; "Svali" said the same things you did and more; also ex Illuminati member Tom something said the same things as you; and both Svali and Tom something are dead. The Illuminati members are going to kill you for sure, just like everyone else who has spoken against the Illuminati before. Please leave the country if you can; go underground if you can. Many whistleblowers who have spoken against the Illuminati are out in the desert living in trailers; there are approximately three communities; all anti-government, anti-Illuminati, all hiding in the desert. Good luck, my friend!

DM: I will be saying many things soon; many things you do not know. **May 15, 2012 at 6:36pm** ·

Videos of Donald Marshall

Donald Marshall is the sword "Anonymous" will use to cleave the Illuminati asunder

3SG1: I may not be there with you in the physical form, but I will be there for you spiritually. Stay strong. These people cannot and will not win! You are stronger than those cowards, Donald.

3SG2: Thank you 3SG1. The interview was done 'on the fly' [in other words: quickly, without thinking and planning what would be done]. The interview features me, Donald and "Anonymous" ("We Are Legion"). The interview is uncut and part 1 will be on YouTube tomorrow.

3SG1: I am looking forward to seeing the video interview of Donald. "Anonymous" ["We Are Legion"] has always got my vote. I support Anonymous and the war against the Illuminati.

DM: I am the sword that "Anonymous" ("We Are Legion") will use to cleave the Illuminati asunder. There are many people getting ready to talk about the Illuminati REM driven cloning subculture now. The Illuminati are scared of polygraph tests and digging themselves deeper [finding themselves in a more difficult situation]... The polygraph tests must be independent polygraph tests though. The polygraph tests must be independent because the Illuminati have a man from the Halifax Police Department who is loyal to the Illuminati. This man attends the cloning center *as a REM driven clone version of himself* and he will give a false reading for the Illuminati members; the Illuminati are ready for the polygraph tests they will have to face, and therefore have placed their own people in positions to falsify polygraph results for the Illuminati members. *As REM driven clone version of myself at the cloning centers* when I said to the Illuminati *REM driven clones* "No guys. Independent polygraphs" and I laughed, this is when the other Illuminati *REM driven* clones all looked at Queen Elizabeth II *(as a REM driven clone version of herself at the cloning center)* and *as a REM driven clone version of herself at the cloning center* Queen Elizabeth II was stuttering. *Laughter*. The Illuminati members who attend the cloning center *as REM driven clones of themselves*, such as the man who works for the Halifax Police Department who is willing to falsify polygraph results for the Illuminati, was the Illuminati's 'ace up their sleeve' [secret knowledge which would give the Illuminati an advantage]... it is all the Illuminati had in an attempt to beat the polygraph tests.

Furthermore, my relatives who attend the cloning center *as REM driven clones of themselves*, and remember their experiences, have said to me *when we were REM driven clone versions of ourselves at the cloning center* that "They wouldn't even ATTEMPT to lie on a polygraph test. They will readily admit everything once confronted with a polygraph test". It will be over then. I still have so much to say on camera too... a lot... **May 11, 2012 at 4:40pm ·**

The anticipation for Donald Marshall's video disclosures

3SG1: Donald, I am eager to see that video!

DM: I wasn't looking my best when I made the video; I had just woken up and had not shaved in a few days... then I talked about the Robert Pickton murders and I got very shaky and I started to stutter picturing the incident all over again. In the next interview I will be exposing more of what the Illuminati have done, as well as what they do as *REM driven* clone versions of themselves at the cloning center. I will be making more videos on my own at home as well... then I will post the videos on Facebook. **May 11, 2012 at 6:19pm** ·

3SG2: I await the video. Take care!

DM: I will be making more videos from home. My buddy is going to show me how to upload videos and documents from my BlackBerry Playbook tablet. I am still in the process of figuring out the tablet... **May 12, 2012 at 2:51pm** ·

3SG2: I am so glad you got BlackBerry.

DM: Me too. It is a Godsend. **May 12, 2012 at 6:58pm** ·

3SG3: Is the video good quality; lighting, etc?

DM: The videos I am making will be good quality. I am making a video recording tonight from my place. My buddy will help me upload the video once the video is completed for you guys tomorrow. I will make sure I speak clearly and loudly and have a lamp positioned so that everyone can see me clearly. The video recording quality on this tablet is amazing. **May 12, 2012 at 4:11pm** ·

May 12th 2012

Donald Marshall makes a Facebook post regarding his upcoming video disclosure

DM: Tonight, I will be making a video recording which will feature me. I will upload this video recording as soon as possible. Keep up the good fight; we are going viral people; (((("On the upside of a downward spiral, my document went viral!"))); that is the original lyric I sang as *REM driven* clone at the cloning center for the song "Drive by" later performed "Train" (TrainVEVO 2012). The Illuminati *REM driven clones* later changed that part of the song to "On the upside of a downward spiral, **MY LOVE** for you went viral..." and then the Illuminati members got annoyed when people said that: "He sounds like he is singing about a sexually transmitted disease (STD)" *Laughter*

3SG1: Try not to add too much background music. The video should be an organic video as opposed to a 'produced' one.

DM: I am not going to add music. I will just be facing the camera and I will be sitting and talking. **May 12, 2012 at 7:41pm** ·

Donald Marshall uploads a new video to his Facebook timeline

[Find the link to the same video uploaded on Donald Marshall's Facebook timeline (on May 13th 2012) in this document in the reference section, available on YouTube (Eric Hastey 2012a)]

Donald Marshall added a new video: May 13th 2012

The video discusses the Megadeth album cover (2001) and the seriousness of the Illuminati's REM driven cloning subculture; as well as, urging the populace to learn and understand the Illuminati's REM driven cloning and keep informing the public about the Illuminati's REM driven cloning subculture (see Eric Hastey 2012a, in the reference section for further details).

DM: No mask needed [in reference to "Anonymous" (We Are Legion) posters] **May 13, 2012 at 7:18pm** ·

3SG1: It is nice to see you face and hear your voice, Donald. You are doing great. Hang in there and keep your head up! Stay positive my friend. You are protected and guided way more than you know.

DM: Thank you. I'll make longer videos with more information in the future. **May 13, 2012 at 7:49pm**

3SG2: Your hair part in this video (Eric Hastey 2012a) does not match this picture below; but it does seem match the picture below of Dave [Mustaine]...also, your bottom lip does not look as "thick" as this picture [below], or as Dave's [Mustaine's] shown below and your ear appears to protrude more from your head in the video (Eric Hastey 2012a)... Lastly, looking at your nose in the video (Eric Hastey 2012a), it appears to point down at the end or tip, whereas the picture or Dave Mustaine's picture below does not.

DM: 3SG2, that was pathetic...**January 2, 2014 at 8:55pm** ·

3SG3: I am confused. Did you say in that video you uploaded that you do not drink [alcohol]?

DM: Yes when that video was made [May 2012], I did not drink [alcohol]. I drink [alcohol] these days. **January 2, 2014 at 9:06pm** ·

May 14th 2012

Video Disclosure Progress

DM: The latest video I have made is forty-five minutes long and it will take approximately four hours to upload here at McDonald's. I do not think McDonald's will let me hang around here that long. I am also trying to answer all the messages I have received in my inbox; I am also answering many questions which have been asked in threads... There are many concerned people joining our legion. I went home earlier and relaxed a bit and ate, and my heart calmed down. I still feel weak and poorly from the torture of my *REM driven* clones at the cloning center. It will be good when I have Wi-Fi internet connection at home... then I'll have internet connection 24/7. Hopefully I can get Wi-Fi connection at home installed soon.

May 15th 2012

Video Disclosure Progress

DM: I am at a buddy's place on his Wi-Fi internet. I am currently making a video and I will upload the video tomorrow... Keep spreading the truth about the Illuminati's REM driven cloning subculture my friends. Also for those that have not seen it, I will repost the original letter about human cloning and the Illuminati's REM driven cloning subculture.

3SG1: That is great, man. Keep those videos coming Donny. People will see as I did how genuine you are.

Video Disclosure Progress

DM: I am currently uploading a short video. There will be more to follow, where I will detail longer more informative information. However, longer videos take approximately four to five hours to upload. Therefore, until I get Wi-Fi internet connection (which should be soon), the videos I upload will be short in length.

Donald Marshall uploads a short informative video to his Facebook timeline

[Find the link to the same video uploaded on Donald Marshall's Facebook timeline (on May 16th 2012) in this document in the reference section, available on YouTube (Astral 7sight 2014)]

May 16th 2012

Donald Marshall added a new video: Replacement video.

The video is very short in length and tells the viewer Donald Marshall will be making longer more informative videos in the future. (Astral 7sight 2014)

3SG1: You look like Charlie Sheen, I am telling you.

DM: *Laugher* Pre-crack [cocaine] Charlie Sheen I hope... I am sorry the video is so short. Even a video which is only seven to eight minutes in length takes a long time to upload. However, once I have Wi-Fi internet connection at home I will upload longer more informative videos while I sleep. **May 16, 2012 at 5:41pm ·**

3SG2: Nice to "see" you again.

3SG3: Where is your tooth, Donald?!

DM: Ha-ha, I was sick in this video. I forgot I had made this video. My tooth got broken in a street fight [in real life] *laughter*; the tooth got broken diagonally; my opponent got a hit though and I still won. **December 7, 2012 at 4:46pm ·**

3SG4: Hey Don, I must say it is nice to see you. I cannot wait to for your longer video(s). Be well mate; I'm trying to be.

3SG5: You look really good, Donald.

Facebook Posts: The progress of Donald Marshall's Mission

April 26th 2012

Facebook post: Continue spreading the truth about REM driven cloning

DM: Continue spreading the truth about the Illuminati REM driven cloning subculture and everything I have disclosed my friends. You are making a difference and I appreciate every effort you make more than you realise. The Illuminati fear large numbers of the public demanding answers en masse about their REM driven cloning subculture; let's see if we can make that happen.

May 10th 2012

Facebook Post: Donald Marshall still lives and will be making a video disclosure soon

DM: I am still alive. I will post a status update tomorrow. I will also be posting the video recording of me soon. I have the means to fight back more effectively now. Thanks to decent people in the world. **May 11, 2012 at 3:30pm**

May 11th 2012

Facebook Post: Donald Marshall will have Wi-Fi connection soon

DM: I have a "BlackBerry PlayBook" now. I am getting Wi-Fi connection next, and then hell hath no fury...

May 12th 2012

Facebook Post: Donald Marshall informs his friends to keep spreading his disclosures

DM: I am piggybacking signal outside the closed library. Keep up the fight heroes. I am talking to you in threads. I will also be making videos from home soon and then uploading them.

May 14th 2012

Facebook Post: Donald Marshall asks his Facebook friends to "copy and paste" his posts

DM: Lastly, can you guys "copy and paste" my numerous updates to each room / group for me? I am on a device which unfortunately is not allowing me to "copy and paste" right now...

3SG1: You have a big team on your side now, Don. We have already spread this [information about the Illuminati's REM driven cloning subculture] far and wide. Your captors are in serious trouble if they try to hurt you. A large number of people will jump on them fast if they do anything serious to you. HOLD ON AND KEEP TELLING THE TRUTH.

DM: I will persevere and increase the information flow. **May 14, 2012 at 8:45pm ·**

DM: I will be at the library from 10 A.M. tomorrow and will talk to people online from that time. Hopefully, I will not be activated as a _REM driven_ clone at the cloning center when I go to sleep tonight. However, I will keep you all posted on the latest developments. Moreover, once I have Wi-Fi internet connection at home I will disclose information constantly! It will be accurate detailed information concerning all that the Illuminati members do.

Everyone who keeps up to date with the information I disclose, will soon know many accurate, factual and valuable information which has been proven to me clearly by the Illuminati _REM driven clones_ as facts and realities of life, over the many years I have been unwillingly activated as a _REM driven_ clone version of myself at the cloning center whereby the Illuminati _REM driven clones_ shared many of their secrets with me _as REM driven clone versions of ourselves_, in attempts to impress me and brag to me, whenever I was _activated as a REM driven clone version of myself_ at the cloning center. Soon everyone who keeps up to date will know everything that I know which has been plainly proven to me as fact, and because I am one of the biggest sceptics in the world, the Illuminati _REM driven clones_ always had to prove things to me _(when I was unwillingly activated as a REM driven clone version of myself at the cloning center)_ many times over, detailing how each function etc. works to me, before I could accept whatever they said as true and not misinformation. It is a lot of content; however, you'll know everything that I know, soon.

Queen Elizabeth II continues to torture REM driven clones of Donald Marshall

3SG1: Tell them [the Illuminati REM driven clones] that if they hurt you I will get very mad!

DM: _As a REM driven clone version of herself at the cloning center_, Queen Elizabeth II did hurt me when I was last activated _as a REM driven clone_ at the cloning center... Queen Elizabeth II _as a REM driven clone of herself_, hurt me when I was a _REM driven_ clone of myself at the cloning center... unexpectedly... After the previous time I was activated as a _REM driven_ clone and many _REM driven_ clones at the cloning center voiced that they no longer wanted to attend the cloning centers _as REM driven clone versions of themselves_, I thought I might be clear of the place and would no longer be activated _as a REM driven clone_ at the cloning center... I was wrong. Recently, _as a REM driven clone of herself at the cloning center_, Queen Elizabeth II paralysed my _REM driven_ clone (which is easily done on a remote control at the push of a button) and Queen Elizabeth II _as a REM driven clone of herself at the cloning center_, stabbed my _REM driven_ clone for many hours when I was activated _as a REM driven clone_ at the cloning center. _As a REM driven clone at the cloning center_, I lost track of time, as Queen Elizabeth II continued stabbing a paralysed _REM driven_ clone version of me. Time appeared to move very slowly as Queen Elizabeth II _as a REM driven clone version of herself_ continued stabbing a paralysed _REM driven_ clone of me. After stabbing a paralysed _REM driven_ clone of me multiple times, and as a wounded and paralysed _REM driven clone_ I went into a state of delirium... and then Queen Elizabeth II _as a REM driven clone version of herself_ said something at the end of my state of delirium that I did not understand or hear because my consciousness faded from that _REM driven_ clone body. When I woke up from sleeping _in my original (real) body_, I was feeling sick _in my original (real) body_ from the torture carried out on my _REM driven_ clones, because consciousness is linked (Petkova and Ehrsson 2008; Ehrsson 2013).

DM: I had to lay down on my back awake for two hours just to calm my heart and go to the library and mail. I was hoping the Illuminati members would give up transferring my consciousness to my *REM driven* clone whenever I went to sleep and reach REM sleep *(90 - 110 minutes after first falling asleep)* and torturing my *REM driven* clones when the Illuminati members activate me *as a REM driven clone* at the cloning center. I was hoping the Illuminati members had given up... **May 15, 2012 at 6:09pm ·**

May 15th 2012

Facebook Post: Donald Marshall's Facebook account starts behaving strangely.

DM: I cannot reply to posts. My Facebook account is getting very weird all of a sudden. I also keep getting knocked offline, and whenever I try and press the "Post" button on Facebook it does not work. Can you guys "copy and paste" this message to the Facebook rooms (and groups) so that people know why I cannot respond?

3SG1: Same [having the same problems with Facebook].

3SG2: Same [having the same problems with Facebook].

3SG2: It is a shame you cannot post [on Facebook] Donald. I hope you can get some relief from your sickness and that your night is a peaceful one.

May 16th 2012

Facebook Post: Donald Marshall is doing his best to respond to ALL messages.

DM: Trust me friends. I am trying to respond to messages in inbox and to questions in threads. I will get round to responding to all of them... There are many people messaging me... more than there have ever been in my entire life... I will answer all. Once I get Wi-Fi internet connection I'll keep up with it all like a full time job and the information will flow and will be constant.

May 16th 2012

Facebook Post: Donald Marshall will soon reveal a secret about Area 51.

DM: I am going home now. When I am online again tomorrow, I will tell everyone a secret about Area 51; it is a truth about Area 51 which was proven to me when I was activated as a *REM driven* clone version of myself. I hope you will not be too disappointed with what I have to reveal about Area 51...

May 16th 2012

Facebook Post: Donald Marshall posts his original letter to the public on Facebook

Donald Marshall posted his original letter to the public about human cloning and the Illuminati's REM driven cloning subculture on his Facebook wall. The link to the original letter can be found in the reference section: (Donald Marshall Proboards 2012).

Satanic Ritual Abuse; Multiple Personality Disorder; and Dissociative Identity Disorder

3SG1: Has anyone ever heard of SRA? In other words, Satanic Ritual Abuse. Survivors and victims of SRA are appearing suddenly, everywhere. These people who are victims of satanic ritual abuse were tortured as children and as adults in real life (their original bodies were tortured and NOT their clones or REM driven clones). Most people who are victims of satanic ritual abuse block the memories, and children tend to fragment into different personalities to deal with the pain and develop Dissociative Identity Disorder (DID) and Multiple Personality Disorder (MPD).

3SG2: Yes, I have read about this [Satanic Ritual Abuse].

3SG1: Most victims of Satanic Ritual Abuse (SRA) begin remembering what happened to them at approximately the age of 25, and the experiences of Satanic Ritual Abuse reappear to the victims in dreams or flashbacks. Some victims of Satanic Ritual Abuse have found good doctors to help "deprogram" them.

3SG3: Oh my gosh! Is this for real [your letter to the public about human cloning and the Illuminati's REM driven cloning subculture]? This needs to be stopped [human cloning and the Illuminati's REM driven cloning subculture must be stopped]! I couldn't even imagine...

DM: Spread this information about human cloning and the Illuminati's REM driven cloning subculture to the four corners of the earth. The only thing the Illuminati members fear is the public demanding answers about human cloning and the Illuminati's REM driven cloning subculture. The Illuminati members also fear the public demanding that individuals who have been involved with the Illuminati's REM driven cloning subculture submit to polygraph tests so that this can be proven clearly for everyone once and for all. The only thing the Illuminati fear is the public discovering the Illuminati's REM driven cloning subculture, because REM driven cloning is what truly exposes the Illuminati. Too many people know about REM driven cloning now for individuals to be targeted by the Illuminati... spread this information about human cloning and REM driven human cloning far and wide people... It is my only hope to escape this technologically driven nightmare (REM driven human cloning). Have the Illuminati killed Tila Tequila yet? **May 16, 2012 at 5:43pm ·**

3SG4: Donald, can you go on Tila Tequila's Facebook page. Tila Tequila is saying somebody has hacked her Facebook page. She is lying; they [Illuminati] made her lie.

3SG1: Tila Tequila was reprogrammed at her last hospital visit. She has MPD/DID.

3SG4: And what is that [MPD/DID]?

3SG5: It used to be called Multiple Personality Disorder (MPD), and it is now renamed as Dissociative Identity Disorder (DID). Tila Tequila certainly seems like she has been mind-programmed and broken down in many ways. Tila Tequila also seems like a strong soul, and hopefully she will live and tell her truths like you are doing, Donny.

3SG1: Study about Satanic Ritual Abuse and how the victims (for which Tila Tequila may be a victim of Satanic Ritual Abuse) develop Multiple Personality Disorder (MPD) and Dissociative Identity Disorder (DID). It may shed some light on Donald Marshall's disclosures about human cloning, and the Illuminati's REM driven cloning subculture, as well as the rituals these people do, for you.

3SG5: Yes, studying Satanic Ritual Abuse does shed light on Donald Marshall's disclosures. I have read extensively on the subject of Satanic Ritual Abuse and it helped me understand as a therapist just how the mind can be broken down and how the compartments and personalities are formed. If you read a book called "Thanks for the Memories" by Brice Taylor (aka Susan Ford), you will begin to see how torture does create multiple personality disorders. Brice Taylor's experiences are horrific and mind-opening / mind blowing.

3SG1: I meant to direct my comment at 3SG4. We responded at the same time, 3SG5.

3SG5: Do a Google search on Brice Taylor's book "Thanks for the Memories". I am sure there is plenty to read there [which you can draw knowledge from with respect to the ritualistic abuse Donald describes]. Be aware that the dark cabal has posted many lies about Brice Taylor –such as she is 'crazy'; that she has 'made things up' etc. Brice Taylor is now a therapist who helps others who have memories which are coming back and are struggling to make sense of the extensive abuse they suffered.

Polygraph Tests

The Public MUST demand: "People who have REM driven clones submit to polygraph tests"

3SG1: It would be good to get hold of an independent polygraph assessor who will be neutral and definitely with no ties to the obvious...

DM: The public must demand that people who have been involved in the REM driven cloning subculture and remember their experiences as *REM driven* clones submit to polygraph tests. Moreover one polygraph test will be all that is needed and I will tell you why. I will accept a polygraph test and I will pass. After passing my polygraph test, I will then point the way to my mother and stepfather who have already stated *as REM driven clone versions of themselves* at the cloning center: "They wouldn't lie on a lie-detector and dig themselves in even deeper." They'll just say "Well what Donny is saying is true, no need to test us."At this point it will be done, and I'll make sure to get their response on video too. Queen Elizabeth II *as a REM driven clone version of herself at the cloning center* was furious when my mother and stepfather said the above, and Queen Elizabeth II *as a REM driven clone version of herself* responded "Oh you will do no such thing...". However the Cohoon family know that the REM driven cloning subculture is soon to be worldwide knowledge and therefore the Cohoon family replied to Queen Elizabeth II *as a REM driven clone version of herself* by stating "Actually, yer majesty we will say that. You can't tell us to go lie on a lie-detector test and incriminate ourselves further; we want to leave [this REM driven cloning subculture] and we want you to leave Donny alone..." Many people are trying to save themselves, and the Illuminati *REM driven clones* are all frantic. **May 13, 2012 at 11:07pm**

May 14th 2012

Steven Joseph Christopher contacts Donald Marshall's relatives

DM: My 'helping friend' Steven Joseph Christopher has contacted a few of my relatives [against my wishes]... Steven Joseph Christopher made contact with my half brother Wayne. My half brother Wayne and his wife attend the cloning center *as REM driven clone versions of themselves.* My half brother Wayne and his wife would like me to be locked up in prison as a method to silence me so that I do not ruin their "clone zone fun". Steven Joseph Christopher also contacted another brother of mine who is memory suppressed *as a REM driven clone,* but this brother of mine knows that REM driven cloning and the Illuminati's REM driven cloning subculture is true. This brother of mine has a wife and a daughter and wants no involvement so far as REM driven cloning and the Illuminati's REM driven cloning subculture is concerned. Once the Geizers or Cohoons hear that I am disclosing everything about REM driven cloning, as well as, the Geizer's and Cohoon's involvement in the Illuminati's REM driven cloning subculture; then the Geizer's and Cohoons may think that they have to respond in real life otherwise they'll appear to look guilty to the public... The Geizers and Cohoons may charge me with slandering their 'good' names... However, the Geizers and Cohoons may just ignore what has been said about them, and their involvement with the Illuminati's REM driven cloning subculture, because the Geizers or Cohoons would not want to be the first to open the can of beans to spill it [in other words, reveal secret information].

Donald Marshall and friends on: Steven Joseph Christopher's actions

DM: I wish Steven Joseph Christopher did not contact my relatives without my knowledge... Contacting my relatives about REM driven cloning; or contacting my relatives about their involvement in the Illuminati's REM driven cloning subculture was Phase Two of my plan. I need more people with me first; I need more people looking and understanding the topic of the Illuminati's of REM driven cloning subculture before contact can be made to individuals who have been to the cloning centers *as REM driven clone versions of themselves* (and remember the experiences once they wake up). **May 14, 2012 at 7:30pm ·**

3SG1: Steven [Joseph Christopher], also known as "Jesus"?

3SG2: Don, cut Steven [Joseph Christopher] off. If he is the Steven [Joseph Christopher] that I am thinking of; the Steven [Joseph Christopher] who thinks he is the new 'Messiah', is that the one? Oh mate! I've got serious words for that b******d! Don, he's a f*****g nutter! Is it that guy that lives in Arizona and wants to build "The New Jerusalem" on Ayers rock; sorry I meant Uluru? He [Steven Joseph Christopher] is f******g nuts mate! Stay well clear of that b*****d!

3SG3: You have better friends than Steven [Joseph Christopher] Donald. I am always around, and now you have many more people that can do more for you than he [Steven Joseph Christopher] does.

DM: Thank you. Steven Joseph Christopher can call himself "SpongeBob" for all I care. *Laughter*. I need all the people I can get who will help me, against the Illuminati members, and the Illuminati's REM driven cloning subculture. Steven Joseph Christopher may have caused complications (in my mission though). If I get locked away for slandering names, continue my friends; set bail. Yes, Steven Joseph Christopher should have consulted me first on that issue (before contacting my relatives). **May 14, 2012 at 8:58pm ·**

Stephen Joseph Christopher: Nice friend. <u>May 14, 2012 at 9:02pm</u>

Stephen Joseph Christopher: You slipped, Don. You fed me to the wolves, Don; that is not what friends do. <u>May 14, 2012 at 9:18pm</u>

DM: No I didn't... I just stated what happened because, if I am in a six foot high by five foot wide prison cell tonight for slandering the (((('good'))) names of the Slimy Cohoons and others, I wanted people to know what happened... <u>May 14, 2012 at 9:21pm</u>

Donald Marshall's primary objective in life and his mission he must complete

3SG2: Donald, do not let Steven [Joseph Christopher] get inside your f******g head mate!

DM: No one can mislead me and get me to believe something is true when it is not at this moment in my life 3SG2... It might sound like I am bragging but I am very resilient now. I have a mind like a steel trap and I have one purpose in this life I must achieve before I die [which is the dismantling of the Illuminati and the shutdown of the Illuminati's REM driven cloning subculture]. I want vengeance against the Illuminati members for what the Illuminati members have done to me *as REM driven clones*, as well as what the Illuminati members have done to other people *(REM driven clones of people, as well as real people, in their original bodies)*. I also want freedom and I want to free others who are also trapped at the cloning centers *as REM driven clone versions of themselves* and save many lives so that the Illuminati members cannot kill these people in the future. I do NOT want fame and I can guarantee that statement is true about me. Money on the other hand will be nice, but it is not necessary. More than anything, I need justice for all that I have suffered, as *REM driven clones and in real life*. I also want to avenge the deaths of REAL people that I was forced to watch their death videos over and over again *as a REM driven clone version of myself* at the cloning center. I do not have interests anymore. I do not appreciate beauty. I begin shaking *in my original body* when I start to think of the things I have seen *as a REM driven clone version of myself*. Those (REM driven clone) experiences are not like daydreams, they are CLEAR experiences, clear like daylight.

Donald Marshall further explains the experience of being a REM driven clone

DM: OH YES PEOPLE, experiences as a *REM driven* clone are CLEEEEAAAR unlike a dream. Dreams are fuzzy and sometimes you do not know you are dreaming or that you have had a dream; dreams are also non-linear and random occurrences. REM driven cloning experiences are not fuzzy at all! As a *REM driven* clone you walk around the same earth, and experience the same earth CLEAR as a bell [in other words, easily understood, like the sound of a bell]. The clarity of the experience I have as a *REM driven* clone is the worst thing. It is SO CLEAR that I when I am activated as a *REM driven* clone version of myself, I even look at the features of my *REM driven* clone at the bathroom the Illuminati have at the cloning center; or I used to look at the features of my *REM driven* clone in the bathroom there every time I was activated as a *REM driven* clone at the cloning center to make a note of the subtle differences between my *REM driven* clone face and my original body's (actual) face... the subtle differences between the eyes; the wrinkles; fingernails; lips; face; the width of my *REM driven* clone body; the height of my *REM driven* clone body compared to my original body etc... It was all fascinating to note; look at; and compare at first... however, the novelty has worn off for me now. I NEVER want to be a clone version of myself of ANY type of clone (Mark 1 to Mark 4 clones; reanimated clones etc.) ever again!

The reasons why: it is NOT great to have sex with public figures as REM driven clones

DM: Furthermore, for anyone who thinks that it might be fun to have their consciousness transferred to their *REM driven* clone duplicate at the cloning center and have *REM driven* clone sex with Rihanna or Brad Pitt... I have news for you: the Illuminati *REM driven clones*, seldom wash the *REM driven* clones they store at the cloning center and most of the time *REM driven* clones at the cloning center smell BADLY. Furthermore, celebrities, megastars and other public figures, have *REM driven* clone sex with **multiple** *REM driven* clones at the cloning center, when these celebrities, megastars and other public figures are *REM driven* clone versions of themselves at the cloning center.

As REM driven clone versions of themselves at the cloning center, the celebrities, megastars and other public figures have *REM driven* clone sex with ANYONE who is also *REM driven* clone version of themselves at the cloning center; that is: if that person can benefit the celebrity, megastar or public figure in real life. If that person as a *REM driven* clone version of herself or himself can benefit the celebrity, megastar or public figure in real life, then the celebrity, megastar or public figure will have *REM driven* clone sex with that person as a *REM driven* clone version of herself or himself –so LONG as the celebrity, megastar or public figure benefits in real life.

As REM driven clone versions, public figures talk down to civilians as if civilians are "fleas"

DM: Moreover with the seldom time spent washing themselves as *REM driven* clones at the cloning centers, the celebrities, megastars and other public figures are ready to have *REM driven* clone sex at the cloning centers as SOON as they are activated. Furthermore, *as REM driven clone versions of themselves at the cloning center* these celebrities, megastars and other public figures think they are above peasants (the public) and will talk down to civilians as if the celebrities, megastars and other public figures are "gods" and civilians are "fleas" and lucky to be in the presence of these celebrities, megastars and other public figures. Even as *REM driven* clone versions, this is how these celebrities, megastars and other public figures treat members of the public who are not famous or well known. *As REM driven clone versions of themselves* these celebrities, megastars and other public figures are greasy headed, inconsiderate, arrogant, scummy people. Moreover, *as REM driven clone versions of themselves*: these celebrities, megastars and other public figures have also watched the murders of REAL children who were brought to the cloning centers; and these celebrities, megastars and other public figures did nothing to help prevent the deaths of REAL children (whether as REM driven clones or in real life with their influence). Some of these celebrities, megastars and other public figures *as REM driven clone versions of the themselves at the cloning center* even cheered and wanted more as these REAL children were being murdered. This is the main reason I was afraid to talk... because it is very difficult to accept that a human being could do such monstrous things to another human being... especially to defenceless children, but that is exactly what the Illuminati members do. Moreover, the difficulty in accepting that human beings can do such monstrous acts to other human beings IS THE ILLUMINATI'S ONLY DEFENCE. So long as the majority of people continue to dismiss the fact that some human beings can be this cruel and evil towards other human beings, the Illuminati members continue undetected to a large majority of the public, and the Illuminati members continue committing hideous crimes against humanity.

The populace MUST investigate Donald Marshall's disclosures DILIGENTLY!

DM: The populace MUST investigate this information carefully, and get past the point where it is difficult to accept that other human beings can be this wicked towards other human beings and reach the point where members of the public KNOW that there is a small subset of human beings who ARE this cruel to other human beings; this is when the Illuminati will no longer have the defence that their malevolent actions are too wicked to be believable. Once the populace knows and understands that some humans can, and ARE this cruel to other human beings, the populace can motion towards having these Illuminati people being investigated publicly and motion towards a point where justice is reached for the crimes committed against humanity by the Illuminati members.

I am going home now. I am having heart lurches as well as other things and I have to lie down. Um help me. Do you know what "beseech" means? I beseech you. Do NOT turn away afraid... or feel helpless to do something... It is your world too. Start by informing anyone you can about the Illuminati's REM driven cloning subculture. **May 14, 2012 at 9:45pm**

"Beseech" [Bih-seech]: "to make an urgent appeal"

Donald Marshall and friends: thoughts on Steven Joseph Christopher continued

3SG4: It should be your choice [when you feel the time is appropriate for you to contact individuals involved in the Illuminati's REM driven cloning subculture; especially if it involves your relatives] Don, not Steven [Joseph Christopher's]. He [Steven Joseph Christopher] overstepped his boundaries. The 'Messiah stuff' is downright creepy! You have a right to do things in your own way [Donald]. I am thinking of you and hoping you make choices that help you! You lose credibility if you let someone who thinks he is Jesus / Messiah, control your life. Why is this situation different from letting Queen Elizabeth II and her gang do it?

3SG5: For sure... anyone who tells me 'they are the Messiah' loses me immediately.

DM: Steven [Joseph Christopher] can go away now. He [Steven Joseph Christopher] is being counterproductive. Steven Joseph Christopher tells everyone he is 'God' [when he is NOT] whenever he is telling people about me, and rightly they know Steven Joseph Christopher is not God, so they dismiss him AND furthermore, they dismiss what I have to say about the Illuminati's REM driven cloning subculture (through association). Steven Joseph Christopher is also editing conversations to make the conversations sound worse than they are actually are. This is something I really could do without in terms of disclosing the Illuminati's REM driven cloning subculture. I do NOT need this! I do not need a retarded person [Steven Joseph Christopher] who is living in his parent's basement with nothing to do but harass me with foolishness. Now because I do not accept that Steven Joseph Christopher is God or Jesus Steven Joseph Christopher said to me "Wrong move a*****e!" as if Steven Joseph Christopher was going to damage me in some way. Steven [Joseph Christopher] the Illuminati *REM driven clones* told me *when I was activated as a REM driven clone version of myself at the cloning center* that "Your parents are Freemasons"... maybe this was your purpose all along. **May 15, 2012 at 6:44pm** ·

Steven Joseph Christopher: *Laughter*. That just shows how stupid you are. They give you misinformation about me. You are gullible... my parents are not Freemasons *Laughter*. Which is it: retard, mason or Messiah? *Laughter*. **May 15, 2012 at 6:48pm** ·

DM: Well it is not Messiah. **May 15, 2012 at 6:48pm ·**

Steven Joseph Christopher: hahhahaha, ya sure, gulligan. **May 15, 2012 at 6:49pm ·**

DM: It is Gilligan Steven [Joseph Christopher], AND I am not Gilligan. I am the "Skipper" [Captain]. You [Stephen Joseph Christopher] ARE Gilligan WANTING to be the skipper, but it is my boat G [gangster / friend]. **May 15, 2012 at 7:24pm ·**

"Gilligan" is a reference to the fictional character "Gilligan" portrayed on the television show "Gilligan's Island". Gilligan was often clumsy, bumbling, dim-witted and accident prone.

May 16th 2012

Facebook Post: Donald Marshall disassociates himself from Steven Joseph Christopher

DM: ATTENTION: Steven (retarded 'god guy') has been blocked from my Facebook account. Please disregard any future posts by Steven Joseph Christopher about me as he is a schizophrenic. I saw him and his website as a way to spread the letter. I didn't know his mind was that far gone. I apologize to anyone Steven Joseph Christopher has offended. He will most likely turn negative. Ignore Steven Joseph Christopher; he is irrelevant. Again I am sorry. I thought I could use all the people I could get but Steven Joseph Christopher is counterproductive.

3SG1: It is good that you blocked him.

3SG2: Good move my friend; stay strong.

3SG3: I had an odd feeling about Steven [Joseph Christopher]. I first read your letter (Donald Marshall Proboards 2012) on a forum Steven posted your letter on. I went to Steven's website every day because he posted your letters and Facebook posts. I always disliked the fact that Steven kept trying to call himself the 'Messiah' yet on his original post on the forum he said he and his friends thought you were just a schizophrenic or crazy. I am glad you chose to block him. I did not like that comment Steven left about you being an informant and that you should "get back in line". F*** Steven Donald, he is a nut job [crazy].

3SG4: As soon as I saw that guy [Steven Joseph Christopher] and read his first post, I knew he would only bring negativity to you. He made it all about himself, and that's not what it's about. Glad you did that, Donny.

3SG5: Steven [Joseph Christopher] is not God and he is NOT Christ. The very fact he tries to call attention to himself the way he does is proof of that.

Illuminati Factions

The Chinese and Japanese Illuminati members who attend the cloning centers

3SG1: I still recommend that you travel to China [in order to complete your mission of exposing the Illuminati and their REM driven cloning subculture].

DM: All the richest and most powerful Chinese political heads of China attend the above ground cloning center *as REM driven clones*, in Canada which I unwillingly attend. It turns out these rich, powerful and political Chinese figure heads want to see the white man get tortured [as a REM driven clone] and see the song freak start freestyle singing [as a REM driven clone] to get them to stop torturing him [as a REM driven clone]. **April 3, 2012 at 9:03pm**

3SG1: What about the "Dragons" [have you seen them at the cloning center]?

DM: There are White Dragons from Japan [who attend the cloning center as REM driven clones] there; and the "Yamaguchi-gumi" clan of Yakuza [who attend the cloning centers as REM driven clones]. I have never seen any Chinese groups called "Dragons" though. **April 3, 2012 at 9:12pm**

3SG1: Good. Now go to China and look for the Dragons. If there is any honour left in the Dragons, they are the last ones. They have proven their worth to the world many times over. What have you got to lose?

DM: True [what do I have to lose?]. However, I have no money to travel to China. I can try to contact the Dragons through internet... **April 3, 2012 at 9:16pm**

3SG1: The internet is last place the Dragons would contact anyone. Get the money. Get there. You aren't too far from China. Walk if you have to. Or, die trying.

DM: Walk to China from Nova Scotia Canada? I'd eventually be swimming. And they could still clone me [and transfer my consciousness to the cloning center in Canada] into the place wherever it is located. Even if I were in China, Australia, wherever... [the Illuminati can still clone me and transfer my consciousness to my REM driven duplicate clone wherever in the world I am]. **April 3, 2012 at 9:26pm**

The reptilian-hybrid fallacy

There are NO hybrid-demon-Illuminati-human members. The main topic is "Cloning"

3SG1: The Illuminati are demon reptilians.

DM: OK there are no such things as demon reptilians in the Illuminati or anywhere else. You should avoid saying "demons" because it makes you sound uninformed, and the concept of 'demons' is just misinformation. For example: "Lookout for the half demon Illuminati!" *Laughter*. Primarily all that the Illuminati do is cloning (and REM driven cloning) and if there were real demons THEY (The Illuminati) would know about them and the Illuminati would have showed me. The Illuminati have already showed me EVERYTHING *as REM driven clones at the cloning center*. They have showed me every technology which they have at the cloning centers *(as REM driven clone versions of ourselves)* in attempts to try and impress me or brag, and in the hope to get me to willingly join the Illuminati. It is CLONING! That is all the Illuminati are about. It is NOT magic or anything else. It is cloning and technology; highly advanced technology, hidden and secret. HEY, watch out for those demons; the horns are sharp! Try your best to avoid saying demons, because it is mainly cloning (and REM driven cloning) the Illuminati are involved with. **April 24, 2012 at 7:59pm**

The Illuminati members are human and they are perverts!

3SG1: Donald, the Illuminati are demonic. How can you say demons don't exist?

DM: Yes well... since the Illuminati released my *REM driven clone* memories back to me, I have evolved in my thinking, and I now know all that they do and are capable of, and therefore I have no choice but to inform the world about the true nature of the Illuminati. The Illuminati are not demons. The Illuminati are perverts. The Illuminati are NOT reptilian aliens (reptilian-alien-hybrid-humans; –they are humans). The Illuminati members are cowardly diddlers who hide in the dark. That is all. The Illuminati members have a lot of money and hide in the dark with their highly advanced technologies.

Your heart is in the right place. At least you do not like the Illuminati and the NWO, so that is a plus for you. Trust me, there are no demons. The Illuminati would have told me *as REM driven clones at the cloning center when they activated me there* if demons were real. The Illuminati bragged to me about every piece of technology which they have, and all the knowledge the Illuminati have acquired *-as REM driven clone versions of ourselves at the cloning center*. I'll tell you about all the technology which the Illuminati have and the facts the Illuminati shared with me and unequivocally proved to me as fact *–as a REM driven clone at the cloning centers*. **April 24, 2012 at 9:22pm**

Donald Marshall on: the misinformation of "demons" perpetuated by the Illuminati

3SG1: Demons are real Donald, and the Illuminati meet at the Bohemian Grove.

DM: OK. Give it up with the 'demon stuff' you sound like little kids. Also the Bohemian Grove... yes the Illuminati are very good braggarts... It is all the Illuminati talked to me about _as REM driven clones at the cloning center_ (what they have done and what they can do). Now the Illuminati members do not tell me sensitive information when I sleep and reach REM sleep (90 -110 minutes) and I have my consciousness transferred from my original body to my _REM driven_ clone and I am a REM driven clone at the cloning center... because once I wake up from sleeping, I tell the whole world exactly what the Illuminati do and what the Illuminati will be doing. You seem 100% sure that demons exist; well you must have seen a demon then... *laughter* I can say I am 100% sure about the REM driven cloning subculture with confidence; I can say with 100% confidence regarding the songs I have made at the cloning centers as a REM driven clone; I can say with 100% confidence about the people in the public eye who are paedophiles _at cloning center as REM driven clones_... and everything else I have witnessed firsthand _through the process of consciousness transfer to my REM driven clone at the cloning centers_... but demons dude? Come on... you know the Illuminati put that misinformation into the public, to mislead the public into believing demons exist and throw the public of the main trail: which is cloning, REM driven cloning / the cloning centers. REM driven cloning is the main secret the Illuminati hold. I know many facts regarding the topic of REM driven cloning, and soon you will too. Document2 is getting made soon. **April 25, 2012 at 4:14pm**

Donald Marshall on: the knowledge he gained from the Illuminati factions / members

3SG1: Donald, the Illuminati really tell you everything they do?

DM: Yes. The Illuminati members told me everything _as REM driven clone versions of ourselves_ at the cloning center. I had the highest rank. I was hanging there as a _REM driven_ clone at the cloning center with all the highest ranked Illuminati members _as REM driven clones_. All that these high rank Illuminati members ever talked about _(as REM driven clone versions of themselves at the cloning center)_ was what they have done and what they can do; bragging and trying to impress me. "Slave 1" I was called (but if you want to get on with me –**never** call me "Slave", "Slave 1" or any variety of "Slave" – I **HATE** it, and it brings up intense negative emotions for me because of being trapped as a REM driven clone at the cloning centers for over 30 plus years, so avoid it at all costs if you want us to get on) but a valued slave, and an amazing person to the Illuminati, that the high rank Illuminati members wanted to talk to all the time and hang with. The problem is I am not evil... **April 24, 2012 at 9:47pm**

The Illuminati members are NOT reptile-human hybrids, the Illuminati members are humans

3SG1: Queen Elizabeth [II] must be a reptile hybrid.

3SG2: I think few people think this too. I have friend who has pictures of her, where he highlights parts of her body that are losing the human look so to speak.

DM: OK. Let me clear this up: the Illuminati members are NOT reptiles; they are humans. Queen Elizabeth II is just very old and Queen Elizabeth II is getting extremely haggard. Queen Elizabeth II is human. Do NOT waste your time thinking the Illuminati members are reptiles, demons, or aliens –they are not; they are human. The main topic regarding the Illuminati is cloning: human cloning, REM driven cloning etc. It is cloning. The Illuminati members LIKE it when people are talking about the other topics; the Illuminati THEMSELVES even throw some misinformation into the mix; the Illuminati release misinformation in movies and other media which influences popular culture to keep the public thinking about the possibilities; make the public think ANYTHING; as long as it is NOT human cloning and REM driven cloning; and definitely make sure the public do not start asking any questions about cloning and REM driven cloning. However, it is cloning and REM driven cloning. Therefore "cloning" is the main topic the public should **focus** on concerning the Illuminati. **April 27, 2012 at 7:59pm**

3SG3: The serpent has been with the royal family for a very long time... [This comment was made with reference to Queen Elizabeth I's four hundred year old portrait which was revealed to show Queen Elizabeth I holding a snake (Daily Mail, 2010)]

DM: Stop it with the reptiles. Queen Elizabeth II probably has a few scales on her butt, but other than that there are no reptile-human hybrids in the Illuminati. The snake symbolism represents Lucifer: "The light bringer" as the Illuminati calls Lucifer. **April 29, 2012 at 10:35pm**

Donald Marshall on: Scotland and Scotland's involvement with the Illuminati

3SG1: Scotland is in on the battle! Illuminati! You better run!

DM: Scotland is IN the Illuminati. Duke Philip, Queen Elizabeth II's husband runs the lodge of Freemasons in Scotland. Do not look for Scotland to help you against the Illuminati. Scotland is a part of Great Britain. Great Britain is the capital of the Illuminati. **April 22, 2012 at 6:11pm**

Donald Marshall on: the Illuminati's best guarded secret: REM driven cloning

3SG1: Is everyone in [the Illuminati] that industry someway connected or understand the depth of what you speak of? Or is it [REM driven cloning] subtle to most?

DM: All involved are connected through REM driven cloning. That is how they meet in **complete** secrecy, through REM driven cloning technology, through the process of consciousness transfer from their original body to their _REM driven_ clone when they go to sleep. REM driven cloning is one of the Illuminati's best guarded secrets. REM driven cloning is 32nd Degree Freemasonry knowledge, which I am giving to the world for free because REM driven cloning is the topic which TRULY exposes the Illuminati. The ONLY thing the Illuminati members fear is the populace learning about their REM driven cloning subculture and the populace demanding the Illuminati members submit to polygraph tests. REM driven cloning is the topic which TRULY exposes the Illuminati, and the Illuminati are frantic now! This is the most the Illuminati have ever been concerned about being exposed. **May 2, 2012 at 5:53pm ·**

The Illuminati's fate once the world grasps The Illuminati's REM driven cloning subculture

3SG1: DEATH TO THE ILLUMINATI! DEATH TO THE NEW WORLD ORDER!

DM: Sounds good to me. Soon the public will start asking questions; demanding answers; asking "If their children have been cloned?" When the public start demanding answers, the Illuminati members will not be able to stem the tide [stop the cause] and the Illuminati will be forced to disclose their nefarious deeds and hope for mercy from the angry, disgusted world. The Illuminati members will act meek, afraid, and ashamed and try and take me down with them [include me as a complicit member in their REM driven cloning subculture]. The Illuminati members will show the world edited footage of me drugged as a _REM driven clone_, while saying this or that... A few times in the past, _as a REM driven clone version of myself at the cloning center_ the Illuminati forced me, and MADE me _as a REM driven clone_ say certain things on camera... As a _REM driven clone at the cloning center_ I was forced to say things that people who are uniformed about the Illuminati's REM driven cloning subculture would view the footage and hate me badly for having said those things... Furthermore, if I did not say those things, the Illuminati _REM driven clones_ would have torn me apart and tortured my _REM driven_ clones over and over... These days _when I am activated as a REM driven clone version of myself at the cloning center_, I do NOT say any of the unwarranted things the Illuminati _REM driven clones_ would like me to...

How Donald Marshall currently behaves when he is activated as a REM driven clone

DM: These days, *as a REM driven clone version of myself unwillingly activated at the cloning center*, I just make a tune for the night; I ONLY make one song for the night, these days and nothing else; and as a reward for the night the Illuminati *REM driven clones* deactivate my *REM driven* clone, so that my consciousness no longer inhabits my *REM driven* clone during my sleep, and I no longer have to be a *REM driven* clone at the cloning center until I wake up *in my original body* from sleep. As a reward for making a song as a *REM driven* clone *at the cloning center* for the night, the Illuminati *REM driven clones* deactivate my *REM driven* clone, and 'let me go' for the night. However, sometimes *as a REM driven clone version of myself at the cloning center*, I smack the Illuminati *REM driven* clones and then the Illuminati *REM driven* clones attack me. I smack the Illuminati *REM driven* clones, because the Illuminati *REM driven* clones are going to attack me anyway. Other times, *when I am activated as a REM driven clone at the cloning center*, I do not even listen to the Illuminati *REM driven* clones' first sentence, I'll just start smacking. Most times *when I am activated as a REM driven clone at the cloning center* I'll just pull a running jump-kick or smack the Illuminati *REM driven* clones in the face over and over... as much as possible... In the past, *when the Illuminati would activate me as a REM driven clone at the cloning center* I would punch their *REM driven* clones, but after a while, *as a REM driven clone version of myself*, my hands will break; and once my hands are broken as a *REM driven* clone, I become useless fighting. Other times when *I have been activated as REM driven clone version of myself at the cloning center, and* I have been attacked by the Illuminati *REM driven* clones; *then, as a REM driven clone version of myself at the cloning center,* I will pretend to be defeated and scared for a while... until I can get close to Prince Charles of Wales *as a REM driven clone version of himself at the cloning center* or any of the ringleaders of the cloning center and *SMACK* -*laughter*. Smack, smack, smack! During this moment, someone in the control room of the cloning center pushes a button and I fall to the ground paralysed as a *REM driven* clone version of myself... this is when the Illuminati *REM driven* clones start beating me in the face as a *REM driven* clone version of myself at the cloning center... it is the same old monotonous idiocy, over and over again. It is the league of incredible super diddler losers! **May 12, 2012 at 3:45pm**

May 12th 2012

Donald Marshall on: McDonald's

DM: I am now on free Wi-Fi internet connection at McDonald's... even Ronald McDonald is helping me stop the Illuminati / New World Order (NWO).

3SG1: Yes but do not eat the 'food' for Christ's sake, or you really will be in trouble!

DM: Strawberry banana smoothies are good though... **May 12, 2012 at 5:51pm**

3SG1: The fries are good too! Come to think of it, so are the hash browns. I quite like the milkshakes too.

3SG2: I don't think so. All the chemicals McDonald's pump into that food will not help us to make it through the photon belt... Research how McDonald's make chicken nuggets, and that will give you the tip of the iceberg of what it is like to serve S**T to consumers; and better yet consumers love their McDonald's [even though it is not good for them]; the consumers revel in it [even though they should not].

DM: True. Even McDonald's burger buns have addictive ingredients in them; and McDonald's are allowed by law to put addictive ingredients in their burger buns. Furthermore, **McDonald's meat** is mostly chopped up guts; and McDonald's then say it is "100% beef only" –because that **was** the name of the meat rending plant they used ("100% Beef")... very clever. McDonald's meat is mostly chopped up guts and eyeballs. McDonald's is the biggest purchaser of cow eyeballs in the world. *Laughter* McDonald's has got their eyes on you! *Laughter* **May 13, 2012 at 8:14pm** ·

3SG3: McDonald's are also loaded with Freemason symbols. The arches for their symbol "M" (for "McDonalds") are a dead giveaway.

DM: The people that own McDonald's are ALL Freemasons; including the Japanese who own McDonalds; the Japanese people who own McDonald's are also Freemasons. The owners of McDonald's also attend the cloning centers *as REM driven clone versions of themselves*; and *as a REM driven clone version of myself, at the cloning center*, the owners of McDonald's asked me *when I was a REM driven clone at the cloning center* to come up with slogans for McDonald's... "(((I'm lovin' it)))" (Filipe Augusto 2007; justintimberlakeVEVO 2009) is a slogan which I coined at the cloning center *as a REM driven clone version of myself at the cloning center* and McDonald's had Justin Timberlake sing it... Although I said that line though... *(as a REM driven clone version of myself at the cloning center)*. The owners of McDonald's always used to bother me for ideas... even at the age of five or six when the Illuminati grew duplicate clones of me and I was first activated as a *REM driven* clone at the cloning center. **May 13, 2012 at 10:36pm**

Save Donald Marshall from the biggest cult the world has ever seen!

3SG1: Donald, have you seen grey aliens or reptiles there [at the cloning center]?

DM: No, there are no grey aliens. The reptiles? Well, discussing the reptiles is in Phase Three of my disclosure regarding my firsthand experiences as a *REM driven* clone. I will discuss the reptiles when I have a larger audience and feel safer (in respect to my life). We are in Phase One now (disclosing clones, cloning, and the Illuminati's REM driven cloning subculture). To everyone reading this information: get me more eyes before the Illuminati kill me please... I am so afraid for my life... I mean *as a REM driven clone at the cloning center*, I fight at the cloning center valiantly while I can... but a full grown man in real life scared to death... it is embarrassing... it is so heavy [the Illuminati's REM driven cloning subculture]...it is so many things [involving the Illuminati and their REM driven cloning subculture]... I thought the Illuminati's REM driven cloning subculture would have been known by now or I would be dead... I am feeling so sick constantly from heart and head-rushes due to *REM driven* clone torture at the cloning center *(because consciousness is linked and therefore torture of my REM driven clones, affects me in my original body)*... God save me from the biggest cult the world has ever seen! **May 14, 2012 at 9:06pm**

3SG2: Yes Donald, we'll get you more eyes... [to look at this information and the Illuminati's REM driven cloning subculture] this is WAR!

Legitimacy

Why Donald Marshall lives and why his Facebook account has NOT been deleted

3SG1: I have to ask something. You say the Illuminati threaten to kill you if you talk publicly about them, but at the same time you claim talking about the Illuminati and what they do is helping. I would have to think that the Illuminati would have gone ahead and killed you already by talking about them this much? It also makes little sense to me, in the respect that someone as "important" as you claim to be against the downfall of the Illuminati would be allowed to have Facebook access? If the Illuminati have the power to run this big scheme, why don't they have the power to shut down your Facebook account? If the Illuminati have ties with everyone, then the Illuminati would have ties with Facebook and the Facebook owners, and the Illuminati could just delete your Facebook account. It just does not seem to add up.

DM: *Laughter*. It makes perfect sense. The Illuminati want me alive for the possibility of making new songs when I am activated as a REM driven clone at the cloning center; they also want to keep me alive for the possibility to use as a torture spectacle to lure the rich, political and celebrity figures, and keep the world of rich people attending the cloning centers *as REM driven clones of themselves*. Furthermore, the Illuminati cannot shut down my Facebook account because Facebook staff discussed this issue *as REM driven clone versions of themselves* with the Illuminati power families at the cloning center and the conclusion which was reached was that "There is free speech and nobody will believe my claims anyway". Well that was the conclusion which was reached at the time, and **WAS** said, but most believe me now.

DM: When this issue was being discussed at the cloning centers, *the REM driven clones of the Illuminati WERE* then going to delete my Facebook account but then decided against it stating nobody will believe me; then people started believing my eyewitness accounts about *REM driven* cloning and the Illuminati, and then the Illuminati *REM driven* clones said it is too late to delete my Facebook account. The *REM driven* clones of the Illuminati members threaten to kill me *(my original body)* all the time *whenever I am activated as a REM driven clone* at the cloning centers. However, I have said too much about the Illuminati and REM driven cloning, and made the Illuminati members so much money *as a REM driven clone version of myself at the cloning centers* to be killed [now nobody kills a man... who is going to make him money –they always protect their investment]. I have mentioned all of this in the letter ("The goose that laid the golden egg"; Donald Marshall Proboards 2012). The Illuminati are not going to kill me; they told me as *REM driven* clones at the cloning centers. The only thing which seems to bother the Illuminati and scare them is me mailing the letter and the upcoming Document2. Oh do you still think that is Dave Mustaine on the Megadeth Album cover "The World Needs A Hero" (2001)? *Laughter* **April 25, 2012 at 5:45pm**

3SG1: I don't know, Don. I guess I would have to ask Dave myself. *Laughter*

Investigate Donald Marshall's disclosures until you reach a point you KNOW it is truth

3SG1: Don I can understand some of what you are saying, however, it is frustrating for me because I have nothing to go on but your word, but I'll hang by you for now though dude! If you are telling the truth Don, I'd like nothing better than to hand your captors a***s to them...

DM: The last thing which I will write for today, before I head home is for you 3SG1. Let me assure you that I am telling you the truth. The Illuminati's REM driven cloning subculture as well as the people involved and everything else I am disclosing and will be disclosing is so crucial, it is of **MONUMENTAL importance**. I do not know how to convey the truth over text but every friend that I have and spend time with knows that what I am saying about the Illuminati and the Illuminati's REM driven cloning subculture is true. My friends also know that I am honest to a fault and I would not lie about something as big and as serious as this. I have nothing to gain. I would also be proven wrong quickly and easily if my statements were lies, and I would also be in so much trouble, possibly even jail time, for slandering names; using a computer to cause a hoax and inciting a public panic if what I am saying is not true. It is illegal to slander names if it is not true; it is illegal to use a computer to incite a hoax on a mass scale which would cause public dissension, and the punishment is either a fine or imprisonment (Public Interest Disclosure Act (PIDA) 1998 section 43B; Enterprise and Regulatory Reform Act (ERRA) 2013 section 17; The Serious Crime Act 2015 section 41 3ZA, Computer Misuse Act (1990) Section 3A).

However, the Illuminati members have told me *as REM driven clone versions of ourselves at the cloning center*; they do not want me to have a day in court. I'll do a LOT of talking that day... and "REM driven cloning" and the "Illuminati's REM driven cloning subculture" will be public record then. The Illuminati members do NOT want that to start. Trust in me; I swear to anything that is holy in this world, and I do not say that lightly... please investigate what I am saying and get to a point where you KNOW what I am saying is the truth... there are many sources out there which corroborate all that I am disclosing. Life references my disclosures (REM driven cloning) and my disclosures references Life (REM driven cloning).

DM: If you take the time to listen to me, and what I am disclosing about the Illuminati and their REM driven cloning subculture, you will start to realise that there hints of human cloning and REM driven cloning widespread throughout life: in music, movies, art, books, etc. REM driven cloning is everywhere it's just that an insider with valuable information has not come forward and told the world what is right in front of their faces before. I really am your only chance to dismantle the Illuminati, with the information I disclose and will be disclosing, such as REM driven cloning and more, because as I've said before *REM driven cloning* is one of the MAIN topics which truly exposes the Illuminati and the Illuminati members. Furthermore when I say the Illuminati members told me nearly everything *as REM driven clone versions of themselves*, I mean nearly EVERYTHING! *As REM driven clone versions of themselves at the cloning center*, the Illuminati *REM driven* clones were always trying to impress me with which ever neat technology they had; soon you too will know about the technology the Illuminati keep hidden because I will be disclosing the technological advances the Illuminati have made too. I'll tell you about a few of the technologies which they Illuminati have, and trust me I am one of the biggest sceptics in the world.

As REM driven clones at the cloning center, the Illuminati *REM driven* clones had to demonstrate each piece of technology to me, telling me how each function works completely before I accepted that such a technology is indeed that advance and a reality. There are many highly advanced technologies which have been made by Russian inventors. There are also many highly advanced technologies which are made by Chinese inventors. The Russians, Chinese and other Illuminati factions have never told the public that they do have such highly advanced technologies present today, but I will be disclosing all the technologies which they have demonstrated to me *as a REM driven clone at the cloning center* and proven to me that the technologies I will be mentioning do in fact exist and are a reality today. Trust me, NONE OF YOU WILL EVER BE DISSAPOINTED IN EVER FINDING OUT THAT THE INFORMATION I AM DISCLOSING IS UNTRUE, AND YOU WILL NEVER HAVE THAT DISAPPOINTING FEELING AS YOU MAY HAVE DONE WITH OTHERS WHO SPOKE OUT AGAINST THE ILLUMINATI, because unfortunately, this time it is all true. The Illuminati's REM driven cloning subculture is true and a reality; a reality which must be stopped. Help me. Just for pity's sake alone, [for the sake of helping another human being] help me! Help me save the world [from the Illuminati's REM driven cloning subculture]. No, I am not being dramatic. If anything, I am not being dramatic enough. Wake the sheeple up my friends. I will make a video as soon as possible. **May 14, 2012 at 10:06pm** ·

Donald Marshall is just relaying his firsthand experiences, he is NOT scaremongering!

3SG1: How about using whatever power you apparently have to address real issues... who cares about why Chris Brown beat up Rihanna?
Donald Marshall, I am calling you out! You are scaremongering!
Do you have any actual contact with Tila Tequila?
Are you a clone?

DM: OK 3SG1, I am not scaremongering. I am just telling the world what I know to be true from firsthand experience; my eyewitness accounts of this highly advanced technology called REM driven cloning, and the Illuminati's REM driven cloning subculture, the people involved in the REM driven cloning subculture, and how someone like me got unwillingly involved in something such as the Illuminati's REM driven cloning subculture, and how as a child I did **NOT** want to get gross with dirty old men as *REM driven* clones and through feeling threatened and being threatened by the Illuminati *REM driven* clones I did anything I could think of to escape being activated as a *REM driven* clone, and avoid torture as a *REM driven* clone; the Illuminati *REM driven clones* were the ones to first suggest that if I have some kind of use, whether I can sing or dance or do anything worthwhile, I could escape the cloning center rather than having to get gross with old men when I was a child *REM driven* clone being activated unwillingly at the cloning center, so I did whatever I could to escape being activated as a *REM driven* clone, which you would do too if you were in such a situation, only to realise that I was in fact making my situation worse, because once the Illuminati *REM driven clones* realised I had a unique talent, the Illuminati members kept activating me as a *REM driven* clone each time I went to sleep *in my original body and reached REM sleep (90 -110 minutes after first falling asleep)* because I had become a source of income for them.

Donald Marshall is NOT the only "idea" REM driven clone trapped at the cloning centers

DM: I am not the only "idea" *REM driven* clone slave; there are many others who are trapped at the cloning centers as "idea" *REM driven* clone slaves for which they are forced to come up with ideas which the Illuminati profits from through the process of consciousness transferred from their original bodies to their REM driven clones whenever these people sleep. These people are memory suppressed. I am NOT scaremongering. I am just telling what I know about this REM driven cloning subculture because my memories have been released to me manually (by the Illuminati REM driven clones) and therefore I am disclosing all I can about the Illuminati's REM driven cloning subculture, which includes the people who have been involved in the Illuminati's REM driven cloning subculture, to save myself from ever being activated as a *REM driven* clone, as well as, save others from being activated as *REM driven* clones; however, they are memory suppressed, or do not understand that their experiences which may seem strange to them are actually *REM driven* cloned experiences and not exactly 'dreams' in every case. I'm looking out for other people as well as myself, and I am NOT scaremongering. Such high advances in science and technology really does exist today.

Donald Marshall is a natural born human and NOT a clone; he has REM driven clones

DM: Accordingly, I am a real person now; a natural born human. I am only a clone, a REM driven clone when I sleep and reach REM sleep. The function of REM driven cloning depends on sleep, and a person reaching REM sleep, because during REM sleep the voluntary muscles (muscles which you move by yourself, such as the arms and legs become inactive so that people do not act out their dreams) shut down (Walcutt, 2013; Sleepdex 2016) and therefore this is a perfect opportunity for consciousness transfer to a REM driven clone, but a person must be in REM sleep *(REM sleep happens: 90-110 minutes after first falling asleep)* before consciousness transfer to the REM driven clone occurs. So, I am a real person when I am awake, and a clone, -a REM driven clone-, when I am activated by the Illuminati (against my will) as a REM driven clone at the cloning center. Sometimes, the Illuminati members skip nights and do not activate me as a *REM driven* clone version of myself at the cloning center. Nobody can be a REM driven clone version of themselves at the cloning without being asleep in their original body, and falling into REM sleep *in their original bodies.* REM sleep is what gives the Illuminati the opportunity to transfer consciousness to the REM driven clone; Tila Tequila included. Tila Tequila knows me from REM driven cloning; we have spoken many times *as REM driven clone versions of ourselves* at the cloning center. If you mean, do we have contact in real life, Tila has not contacted me [on Facebook] yet. If Tila Tequila permanently wants to leave the Illuminati's REM driven cloning subculture [which she too is a part of], she should be the one to contact me, and I will help her, and she may help me too... **May 18, 2012 at 5:04pm**

Donald Marshall on: song making as a REM driven clone at the cloning center

3SG1: Donald, the song "Cuts like a Knife" was written in 1983. You were seven. A seven year old knows about romantic ballads; and the word "astray"? I just want this all to feel right with me [regarding your disclosure about the Illuminati's REM driven cloning subculture and your involvement in making songs as a REM driven clone at the cloning center and popular artists later performing songs which you made as a REM driven clone version of yourself at the cloning center]. I can handle the truth but if there is an ounce of fiction mixed in, well I don't want to have my reservations.

DM: Yes... I did know about romantic ballads and the word "astray" at the age of seven. I watched television A LOT when I was a child and I had a vast vocabulary. Furthermore, I can understand that it seems extraordinary that a seven year old could write such a song, however the phenomenon is called "vasodilation", also known ordinarily as "a massive rush of blood to the head"; "it is when the blood flow to the brain increases under mental stress, through a process called vasodilation – where the blood vessels get wider to allow more blood through" (The Naked Scientists 2009). Coldplay named their second studio album after the science of "vasodilation" and Coldplay's second studio album is called "A Rush Of Blood To The Head".

Humans become capable of extraordinary feats through the process of "vasodilation"

DM: When a human's life is threatened, humans get a massive rush of blood to the head, as well as, adrenaline. Humans then become capable of extraordinary things to save their lives, as well as, the lives of their children. This is basis of how I started making such amazing songs whenever I was activated *as a REM driven clone version of myself* at the cloning center... As a *REM driven* clone child at the cloning center, I felt threatened whenever I had my consciousness transferred *from my original body* to my *REM driven* clone, and I would suddenly "wake up" through the process of consciousness transfer to find myself in a remote location much different than what I remember when I went to sleep, and unable to recall how I got to this remote location sequentially. I was frightened and thought I was kidnapped. Therefore, because I felt that my life was threatened whenever I was activated as a *REM driven* child clone at the cloning centers unwillingly, I would do anything in an attempt to escape from the place. This involved singing and making songs... as well as, anything I could think of to save myself; such a threatening scenario caused a rush of blood to my head as a *REM driven* child clone... The Illuminati *REM driven clones* would also threaten me as a child *REM driven* clone activated against my will at the cloning center, and the threats from the Illuminati members *as REM driven clone versions of themselves at the cloning center* also caused me as a *REM driven* clone child, to have a massive rush of blood to the head; therefore the stress of suddenly appearing and finding myself in a foreign location to me (because I didn't know I was a REM driven clone at the time, and I was also memory suppressed), as well as, the threats by adult Illuminati members *as REM driven clone versions of themselves* towards me as a child *REM driven* clone at the cloning center, gave me tremendous stress; tremendous rushes of blood to the head; and tremendous amounts of adrenaline, to the point where I felt threatened and my life was on the line, and therefore I felt I had to perform extraordinary feats in order to save myself... this is the basis of how I started making songs as a *REM driven* clone version of myself whenever I was activated unwillingly as a *REM driven* child clone at the cloning center. Consequently, the threatening environment and the threats from the adult Illuminati *REM driven clones* towards me worked.

The Amazing Song Boy: "The Royal Minstrel": Donald Marshall

DM: Furthermore, as a REM driven child clone of myself, whenever I couldn't think of a rhyming word or I got stuck in lyric line, the Illuminati *REM driven clones* sometimes helped me with a rhyming word. *As REM driven clone versions of themselves at the cloning center*, politicians especially liked to put in lyrical lines into some of the songs I made *when I was activated as a REM driven clone of myself at the cloning center*. When I got better at making songs on my own *as a REM driven clone version of myself at the cloning center*, I did not need any help from any *REM driven* clones of original people, at the cloning center; and I just made songs on my own at the cloning center, *as a REM driven clone version of myself.* Moreover, *as a REM driven clone version of myself, activated against my will at the cloning center*, I was mostly singing songs to Queen Elizabeth II *as a REM driven clone version of herself* at the cloning center. Queen Elizabeth II *as a REM driven clone of herself* called me "The Royal Minstrel" *and as a REM driven clone version of myself*, I had to face Queen Elizabeth II *as a REM driven clone of herself* whenever I was composing these songs...

DM: Queen Elizabeth II *as a REM driven clone of herself at the cloning center* said "She fell in love with me" but in reality it was just a premise for Queen Elizabeth II *as a REM driven clone* to talk all the time at the cloning center in front of others who attend the cloning centers *as REM driven cloned versions of themselves*.

How Donald Marshall became the most exciting thing at the cloning centers

DM: Queen Elizabeth II *as a REM driven clone of herself* is an attention seeker and likes to show off and be heard. *As a REM driven clone version of myself* I became the most exciting thing at the cloning center when I started to make songs. More celebrities attended the cloning centers *as REM driven clone versions of themselves* to get their chance to see the amazing song making child... and as a result Queen Elizabeth II *as a REM driven clone of herself* had more of an audience to flap her jowls in front of... Then my song making ability was no longer amazing to the Illuminati *REM driven clones at the cloning center*, it was "expected" of me to make songs whenever I was unwillingly activated as a *REM driven* clone at the cloning center... However, when I was older and much braver I told the Illuminati *REM driven clones* "They are disgusting and I want nothing to do with it [their REM driven cloning subculture]!" I also called the Illuminati *REM driven clones* "Heathens" *as a REM driven clone version of myself* at the cloning center, when I was older and much braver; the rapper Ol' Dirty Bastard (real name: Russell Tyrone Jones) called the Illuminati *REM driven clones* "Heathens" too when he was a *REM driven* clone version of himself at the cloning center and the Illuminati members killed him for this. However, with me, I was worth too much money to the Illuminati members for them to kill (in real life) and *as a REM driven clone version of myself*, I lured many celebrities and high profile public figures to attend the cloning center *as REM driven clone versions of themselves* who otherwise would have nothing to do with REM driven cloning, or the Illuminati's REM driven cloning subculture, so instead of killing me (in real life) the Illuminati *REM driven clones* tortured me whenever I was activated as a *REM driven* clone version of myself at the cloning center.

It is "Only a matter of time" until REM driven cloning is fully exposed!

DM: The Illuminati members, as well as other high profile public people who attend the cloning center *as REM driven clones of themselves* and would otherwise have nothing to do with REM driven cloning if it wasn't for the fact that they came to see me make songs *as a REM driven clone of myself* at the cloning center, have all said *as REM driven clone versions of themselves* that if the Illuminati were to kill me now (in my original body, in real life) I would become a martyr, and the Illuminati members and the Illuminati's REM driven cloning subculture would be found out even sooner if the Illuminati were to kill me. It is only a matter of time until the Illuminati's REM driven cloning subculture is fully exposed and everything I am disclosing is proven clearly to the world. Even the Illuminati members THEMSELVES say "It is only a matter of time [until they are fully exposed] and that I will be saved from REM driven cloning due to the efforts of good people like you 3SG1, and everyone else spreading the information about the Illuminati's REM driven cloning subculture everywhere.

Donald Marshall on: his upcoming video discussing REM driven cloning

DM: You will love the upcoming video with my nephew... He is scared to speak publicly *about REM driven cloning*, but he wants to save me *from REM driven cloning*. My nephew has been activated as a *REM driven* clone of himself at the cloning center approximately twenty times... but he has NOT been activated as a *REM driven* clone at the cloning center for many years now since he freaked out when he saw too much blood and gore at the cloning center *as a REM driven clone of himself*. After that incident his parents demanded that their son is no longer activated *as a REM driven clone* at the cloning center. **May 18, 2012 at 6:41pm**

Negative comments:
Others comments on: Donald Marshall's sanity

3SG1: You're insane Donald! This stuff is not happening to you; why are you making up these weird things? You're crazy and you need some serious mental help. I will pray that you don't live the rest of your life in la-la land. Or maybe it's for personal attention?

DM: 3SG1, you are wrong. Everything I have detailed is true. It is just highly advanced science and technology compared to what the population uses –hidden and in secret, used by the Illuminati against the populace. That's it! If you do not want to hear this or help, then block me! Other than that keep quiet! **May 5, 2012 at 7:36pm** ·

3SG2: 3SG1, go elsewhere. Your negativity is not needed. Donald, I have posted the letter. Now more people are going to KNOW [about the Illuminati REM driven cloning subculture]!

DM: Thank you, 3SG2. **May 5, 2012 at 7:36pm**

3SG2: You are welcome Donald. Many have read your letter and accepted your plight; it is an eye opener and it needs to be KNOWN!

DM: Yes, over 90% of people who have read the letter (Donald Marshall Proboards 2012) know it is the truth, and that is more than enough. I will be posting a video recording of me soon. Once you see a video recording of me it will confirm that the picture on the Megadeth Album cover "The World Needs a Hero" (2001) is me... it really IS me! I posed for the picture as a *REM driven* clone version of myself at the cloning center while the Illuminati *REM driven clones* took pictures. I have been told the image of me on the Megadeth Album cover "The World Needs a Hero" (2001) is an oil painting. Keep spreading the truth about the Illuminati and their REM driven cloning subculture. This REM driven cloning subculture must be shut down and the populace must be informed about what the Illuminati members have done: as their *REM driven* clone versions, and as their original selves; as well as the evil acts they have committed against humanity in real life. The populace **MUST** be informed so that such atrocities are never be committed again, especially hidden from the guise of the world. **May 5, 2012 at 7:48pm**

3SG1: You're insane [Donald]!

3SG2: 3SG1, it is alright. You need to go elsewhere... REM driven cloning, and the Illuminati's REM driven cloning subculture is above your head, and below your knees [too difficult or strange for you to understand]. It is just science and technology... anyone can be have their consciousness placed into a *REM driven* clone body of themselves; think of the movie "Avatar" (2009)... this is what is happening.

3SG1: Have you seen proof? Do you know things beyond Mr. Donald Marshall? It's crazy to take one person's words and perceive them as factual evidence. There is no proof. You're not open-minded, you are just gullible. Donald Marshall also claims Ron Paul is at the "cloning center" all the time. I'm removing this insane man, and I hope you soon realize Donald Marshall is a fake "Illuminati Clone".

DM: Everything I have detailed about REM driven cloning and the Illuminati's REM driven cloning subculture is true. It is all true. Remove me as a friend on Facebook 3SG1. Furthermore, Ron Paul DOES attend the cloning center *as a REM driven clone version of himself*; I have seen Ron Paul *as a REM driven clone of himself* at the cloning center. What I am disclosing is just the effects of highly advanced science and technology hidden and secret which currently exist today. My experiences are firsthand eyewitness accounts through the process of consciousness transfer from my original body to my *REM driven* clone when I sleep, and reach REM sleep *(90-110 minutes after first falling asleep)*. That is how advanced technology is today. Think "Avatar" (2009).

REM driven cloning experiences explained: A person LITERALLY "wakes up" as a clone

DM: Furthermore, when the Illuminati transfer my consciousness to my *REM driven* clone, I open my eyes like *Boom* -and it feels like I have been kidnapped for a second, then I remember I am at the above ground cloning center in Canada. REM driven cloning experiences (once a person is allowed to retain the full memories of their REM driven cloning experiences) are not like dreaming; dreams are fuzzy and incoherent. When I open my eyes as a *REM driven* clone it is **CLEAR**, clear like I am talking to you now; and when I am just about to wake up *in my original body* my REM driven clone drops "limp noodle" –as if dead (the REM driven clone at the cloning center) and my consciousness goes from remembering a LINEAR experience here on earth, CLEAR as daylight, at a remote location (the cloning centers), to a moment lasting about a second or two of blurriness before I open eyes in original body to experience the SAME world again, only this time in my original body, CLEAR as daylight! That is consciousness transfer and how it feels to be a *REM driven* clone explained. A person is LITERALLY waking up as a clone (a REM driven clone), to experience the SAME world the person left behind when their original (real) body went to sleep.

The most important distinction about REM driven cloning

DM: The most important distinction about REM driven cloning is that, when I wake up as a clone version of myself (a REM driven clone) I experience the SAME world, which I left behind **when I went to sleep** in my original body. Unlike dreams and dreaming where the experience is random conjecture... different scenarios... and in dreams the events in the timeline are non-linear... and fuzzy... etc... With REM driven cloning, I am waking up as a clone (a REM driven clone) to experience the SAME earth... So yes: In short these experiences are true, and I have met all the people I have detailed as REM driven clone versions of themselves at the cloning center.

Politicians who attend the cloning center as REM driven clone versions of themselves

DM: Moreover, Hillary Clinton also attends the cloning center *as a REM driven clone version of herself.* I have seen Hillary Clinton *as a REM driven clone version of herself* at the cloning center, when I have been *a REM driven clone* at the cloning center. Whoever wins the U.S. Presidential election is **STILL** a member of the Illuminati and New World Order (NWO), and was either involved in the Illuminati REM driven cloning subculture or becomes part of the Illuminati REM driven cloning subculture; this way the Illuminati never loses.

"The Simpson's" reference: The fraudulence of the election system.

DM: The Illuminati even made a Simpson's episode (H.J. Simpson 2015) about the (Illuminati / NWO) election situation, whereby the aliens Kang and Kodos were dressed in costumes and on the surface appeared to look like Bob Dole and Bill Clinton to an unsuspecting crowd; until Homer Simpson lifted off the face masks to reveal that, it is in fact aliens dressed as Bob Dole and Bill Clinton, and their election system is a fraud... because whoever wins is still an alien... *Laughter* The reality of the situation is that whoever wins the U.S. Presidential election is still controlled by the Illuminati, and is part of the Illuminati's REM driven cloning subculture. Everything I have said is true... and there is more. I will be detailing this soon. **May 6, 2012 at 7:04pm ·**

Negative comments regarding Donald Marshall's legitimacy

3SG1: You're a good story teller Dun.

3SG1: It is easy to see that you are lying when it came to watching your video interview (Eric Hastey 2012a; Eric Hastey 2012b; Eric Hastey 2012c). You overemphasise the fact that you're "telling the truth". If you really were [telling the truth], you wouldn't have to put such emphasis on it. As a matter of fact, you wouldn't have to put any attention on the issue. You are a bold liar, and I do not see the reason why you would go through this trouble to fake people out. You now have a free touch-pad from doing so. You have blind minded people believing your lies. I have to ask... why? Message me your answer.

3SG2: Truth is stranger than fiction 3SG1. Keep an open mind.

3SG1: If you have watched his [Donald Marshall's] interview you can see the ticks of a false story; it is absolutely evident in his first video. Once he starts asking you all for donations for the cause that is when his master scheme will come to light. There is an ulterior motivation to making you people think he is being truthful. Keep an open mind to that.

3SG3: 3SG2, you took the words right out of my mouth [in other words, you said exactly what I was going to say before I had a chance to say it, therefore I agree with you very much]. To a critical thinker the information presented on the television as "news" and the information depicted by mainstream media outlets appears "fictional", because there always appears to be another level of information in addition to what is being presented by mainstream outlets. Therefore, it seems obvious that there will be many more levels to the information which we are presented with by (mainstream) media outlets, and therefore many more levels of information to be presented until we reach any place which resembles truth; it is obvious really. Furthermore, whoever made people think: if a person's eyes go this way or that way is based on truth, and that this applies to the entire population is something which I find odd. Just saying. Peace out.

Donald Marshall on: negative comments towards him and the reality of his disclosures

DM: 3SG1, you are a fool! I have already said that this is all true and that it involves highly advanced science and technology in comparison to what the public uses. That is all. It is just highly advanced science and technology [furthermore, Phil Schneider (Schneider 1995; 1996; Open Minds 2011) demonstrated that for every 12 months which passes, military technology advances by a rate of 44 years compared to the technology the public uses. In other words for every 8.29 days military technology achieves 1 years worth of technological advancement relative to what we as the public see or use]. I have also said it is unbelievable that other human beings would do such monstrous things to other human beings, and because the severity of the Illuminati's actions, is so unbelievable to the average person, this is the Illuminati members' only defence. However, once people learn and understand the fact that the Illuminati's REM driven cloning subculture involves highly advanced technology, and that the Illuminati members **REALLY** do all the heinous crimes I have described and more, the Illuminati members will have NO defence. The only thing the Illuminati members fear is: the public realising the true extent of technological advancements available TODAY; the Illuminati members also fear the public learning and realising that the Illuminati's REM driven cloning subculture is a reality and a fact of life, and therefore as a consequence, the public starts demanding answers for REM driven cloning and polygraph tests of the people involved in the REM driven cloning subculture so that this is PROVEN clearly once and for all, because REM driven cloning is what truly exposes the Illuminati members. I am absolutely desperate because I have NO defence against the Illuminati's better technological advancement and cannot block the consciousness transfer from my original body to my *REM driven* clone. I have also mentioned that the only thing which can save me is the populace, and that the only thing which defeats the Illuminati's better technological advancements is the populace. I am absolutely desperate because my life is on the line, as well as, my continued heart health, which results from the torture I suffer as a *REM driven* clone at the cloning center because consciousness is linked.

Donald Marshall's disclosures regard highly advanced science and technology. That is all

DM: If you cannot accept the fact such highly advanced science and technology is a reality and does exist and is available, as well as, the fact that such highly advanced technologies are hidden from the public 3SG1, and you do not want to know then un-friend [off Facebook] and block me. All you ever do is throw negativity. If you are not open to learning, and you want to be negative, and you cannot accept the fact that all that I am disclosing is true... then go away... it is as simple as that. Moreover you are scrutinising my face? You have Ron Paul's picture [on your Facebook profile] and you support Ron Paul, well guess what? Ron Paul attends the cloning center _as a REM driven clone version of himself_ and he will be another Obama. Hillary Clinton also attends the cloning center _as a REM driven clone version of herself_ and will also be another Obama. In the future 3SG1, you are going to look like a fool. If I have anymore negativity from you 3SG1, you are going to have to leave! This situation is **TOO important** to have an Illuminati troll, plant the seeds of deceit among the people that are going to save me from this _REM driven cloning_ nightmare. Now I want to work harder prove REM driven cloning clearly, to make you look stupid. **May 15, 2012 at 9:58pm** ·

REM driven cloning is a reality and a fact of life. Blast through your "cognitive dissonance"

DM: Some people are so scared by the possibility that REM driven cloning is real that they rebel against the truth of the Illuminati's REM driven cloning subculture to deny and pretend everything is ok... It is a psychological defence of a weak mind. **May 15, 2012 at 10:42pm** ·

3SG2: Donald, it is called "cognitive dissonance".

3SG4: I'm sure 3SG1 is a good guy with good intentions; however, his ignorance has left him blind to possibility of other truths outside his current worldview. His ignorance has also left him blind to the possibility of certain facts or situations which could also be true outside his current worldview beyond his reasoning. This is a shame. Sometimes learning something new requires us to first unlearn something old.

May 18th 2012

More negative comments from individuals with "cognitive dissonance"

Grey aliens, scaremongering, and human cloning

3SG1 posted the following (below) on Donald Marshall's Facebook timeline.

3SG2: I have the same hair colour as a guy that I work with... WE MUST HAVE THE SAME FATHER.

I think the only similarity these people have (other than Caucasian blood) is the same hairdresser.

3SG1: This is a joke picture, but I believe you already know.

3SG2: A joke picture, conveniently posted on a jokers Facebook page.

3SG1: Sometimes jokes contain some bits of truth. I was wondering what Donald has to say about it [the picture I posted]. I'm not interested in anyone else's opinions. It's Donald that has a lot to say.

3SG2: Are you joking? You believe what this Donald joker is putting forward? I'm not in a position to mention who or what; but I have access to information which is NOT available on the surface web [it is on the dark web]. I am telling you this: cloning, maybe; but half of what this Donald character is coming out with is pure disinformation. Scaremongering. I will call you [3SG1] a f******g idiot if you believe it [the Illuminati's REM driven cloning subculture].

3SG2: He [Donald] also denies the existence of grey aliens... what a f*****g idiot! There are over fifty documented types of grey aliens! The grey aliens have been in our space–time continuum for what we would consider 'centuries'. PLEASE do not fall for this guy's B/S. If you want some real answers as to what is happening on this planet at the moment and what will happen this year - inbox me.

3SG1: I have never said I believe him. I am just extending my courtesy to him. Everyone deserves a chance to be heard. Unless he's asking for donations, I don't see why he would spend so much of his life to talk about this [the Illuminati's REM driven cloning subculture] unless he is passionate in it.

3SG2: All I can see is an attention whore. He [Donald] is leading people on with the promise of insider information, yet he is not giving it out. And when he does [give information], it is just nonsensical garbage that reads like it has been "copied and pasted" by a five year old.

3SG1: I have been visited by "greys" and "reptilians" through sleep paralysis in the past. Calling out for "Jesus Christ" has permanently stopped them [grey aliens and reptilians from appearing]. But of course you can argue that they [the Illuminati through their highly advanced technologies] are trying to trick me into thinking Christianity is the truth when it is used to control the masses. But in MY HEART, I feel Jesus Christ is the truth; and that is what guides me. Furthermore, the Bible does NOT mention Extraterrestrials (ETs) or grey aliens; so my only conclusion is: that they are demons in disguise trying to trick people into thinking the Bible is irrelevant.

DM: You are a smart man 3SG1. They [most likely the Illuminati, through their highly advanced technologies] MADE you see grey aliens though there are no grey aliens that the Illuminati members know about... grey aliens are misinformation. The Illuminati members want the public talk about grey aliens, or anything else for that matter, anything EXCEPT "human cloning" and the Illuminati members want the public to avoid the topic of "REM driven cloning" and "The Illuminati's REM driven cloning subculture" because it is REM driven cloning which truly exposes the Illuminati... Stay tuned my friends... and in time you will know everything... **May 18, 2012 at 3:51pm ·**

Media

The fallacy of the Michael Fagan incident (1982)

3SG1: I saw a video where some young black man [Michael Fagan] broke into Queen Elizabeth's II bedroom (The Independent 2012). Queen Elizabeth II forgave him [Michael Fagan] and did not press charges. NO ONE can get into that (Queen Elizabeth II's) bedroom. He [Michael Fagan] was one of her boy toys!

DM: The Illuminati staged the event where Michael Fagan broke into Queen Elizabeth II's bedroom. The reason is because the Illuminati members wanted more security, paid for by the government. **April 17, 2012 at 8:14pm**

The fallacy of the elderly woman who broke free from the barricade past police (2010)

DM: Furthermore, the Illuminati also staged another event during Queen Elizabeth II's Canadian visit [to Toronto] (Nguyen 2010). An elderly woman broke free from the barricade and past police at the St. James Cathedral church (Toronto) to hand Queen Elizabeth II a black plastic bag containing a commemorative tea towel. The Illuminati staged the above event completely! The Illuminati members want government security. The Illuminati members will need a lot more security once enough people know about the children who have their consciousness transferred to their *REM driven* clones while they sleep at home in their beds; children who are then tortured, raped and torn apart for sport *(as REM driven clones)* while they sleep *(because of the process of consciousness transfer from the original's body to the REM driven clones)* by Illuminati members regularly as a religion and a lifestyle. It is a sick comment to make I know, but at least I am telling the world about the nefarious crimes committed against them unsuspectingly. **April 17, 2012 at 8:14pm**

MK Ultra

3SG1 Posted "Madness in the fast lane" Swedish Sisters –BBC programme (♦MOONSTORMSATA♦ 2012)

3SG1: Donald, if you have any information on this case... please share your thoughts on this [the 'Swedish twins' who ran into a truck and survived the impact of the truck, as well as, oncoming vehicles on a busy motorway in the UK... –see the reference above, listed in the references section, for the full documentary]

DM: I do [have information on the 'Swedish sisters' case] but I have no time [to detail this right now]. I will explain later; it is a long story involving clones and MK Ultra and how [MK Ultra] is actually done. **May 15, 2012 at 2:23am ·**

DM: The Illuminati *REM driven clones* even do the mind control (MK Ultra) thing on my *REM driven* clone(s) at the cloning center. With the mind control (MK Ultra) technology that the Illuminati members have, the Illuminati members can make anyone who is a *REM driven* clone version of themselves *at the cloning center*, walk, talk, and make any facial expression, as well as, anything else the Illuminati members want the *REM driven* clone(s) to do, when the *REM driven* clone(s) are under the control of the Illuminati's mind control (MK Ultra) technology. Queen Elizabeth II *as a REM driven clone version of herself at the cloning center* used the Illuminati's mind control (MK Ultra) technology on my *REM driven* clones in the past to make me run around the cloning center while I said and did horrible things as a *REM driven* clone version of myself, against my will, under mind control (MK Ultra) technology which was operated by Queen Elizabeth II *as a REM driven clone version of herself* at the cloning center. Furthermore, Queen Elizabeth II *as a REM driven clone version of herself at the cloning center* videotaped all the horrible things I said and did when I was under mind control (MK Ultra) technology, so that if the Illuminati's REM driven cloning subculture is ever fully exposed the Illuminati members will drag me down with them. Moreover, there is no force of will or strength which can make a *REM driven* clone act against the wishes of the programmer controlling the *REM driven* clone through mind control (MK Ultra) technology. The programmer can literally make a *REM driven* clone do ANYTHING against the will of the person who is a *REM driven* clone version of themselves with the mind control (MK Ultra) technology the Illuminati have. *REM driven* clones are easily mind controlled with the MK Ultra technology the Illuminati members have. I will explain in depth... **May 15, 2012 at 7:02pm**

Religion

Donald Marshall on: praying

3SG1: Donald, do you pray?

DM: I have been praying hard dude. I have been praying to no avail. The Illuminati members try to shake my faith too. The Illuminati members call me stupid for believing in "adult Santa Clause". I need world attention now. World attention is what is going to save me. If I die (in my original body) the Illuminati will continue REM driven cloning against the populace, as well as their many despicable crimes against humanity unchecked. The Illuminati must be stopped and the cloning centers must be shut down; and the people responsible for carrying out and continuing these crimes against humanity must be punished. There are so many people at the cloning center *as REM driven clone versions of themselves* that do NOT want to be activated at the cloning centers, and do not want to be there. The people who do not want to be at the cloning centers *as REM driven clones* are just waiting... They are waiting until I get some kind of big attention then they are going to try to save themselves from REM driven cloning as well... However, people who do not want to attend the cloning centers *as REM driven clone versions of themselves* are scared now... After they witnessed the different variations of torture which has been carried out on my *REM driven* clones, and after seeing what the Illuminati members do to me for publicly speaking out about the Illuminati and REM driven cloning, they are afraid of what may happen to them; especially, after the death of Bernie Mac (actor / comedian).

DM: The people who do not want to be at the cloning centers *as REM driven clone versions of themselves* are afraid they will have their lives sabotaged, and ruined systematically by the loyal Illuminati members who attend the cloning center *as REM driven clone versions of themselves at the cloning center.* **April 12, 2012 at 6:15pm**

Why Donald Marshall does NOT like discussing topics to do with religion

3SG1: Donald, how come you do not like discussing any topics to do with religion?

DM: It is because when I am unwillingly activated as a *REM driven* clone at the cloning center, the Illuminati *REM driven* clones throw religious dogma, every second of the day and every opportunity they get, for over the thirty plus years the Illuminati has been activating me as a *REM driven* clone at the cloning center, and because of that I really do **NOT** like discussing religion and I grew tired of talking about religion as a topic. Furthermore, bringing religion to this cause makes this situation more confusing, less easy to understand or deal with. As I have mentioned before, the only advantage the Illuminati members have is a **technological advantage**. It is a technological advantage which the Illuminati hold. The populace learning about REM driven cloning and understanding the Illuminati's involvement in REM driven cloning; and the Illuminati's REM driven cloning subculture, is the world's only hope against the Illuminati's better technological advantages. This is what the Illuminati fears. The Illuminati members fear the repercussions they shall face once a large percent of the population learns and understands the Illuminati's highly advanced technologies for which the Illuminati members keep hidden and in secret and use against the populace for nefarious purposes.

Let's focus on the main topic which TRULY destroys the Illuminati: REM driven cloning

DM: The Illuminati members fear the populace understanding REM driven cloning and demanding answers and polygraph tests because this is what TRULY exposes them. So please, let's focus on the main topic at hand which TRULY destroys the Illuminati: The Illuminati's REM driven cloning subculture. Let's work together guys and better yet, let's NOT make this cause more confusing, and less easy to understand or deal with by adding religion to the mix because it **IS** just a better **technological advantage** which the Illuminati have. It is just science and technology. So let's focus on the science and technology which has been CLEARLY proven to me exists and I know exists because my *REM driven* experiences are vivid, and I am not speculating or guessing. It is REM driven cloning which exposes the Illuminati so please everyone try and stay on this topic; stay on the topic of REM driven cloning. Remember you are bringing down the most enormous, most scummy cult in the world; full of the world's richest and most influential people. The main topic which defeats the Illuminati and the main topic which the Illuminati fear: is the public demanding answers to is REM driven cloning, because it IS REM driven cloning which exposes the Illuminati. Therefore, we HAVE to stay focused on REM driven cloning and stay on this course... we are so close now... fighting, as well as, fighting over religion will only slow our efforts. **May 11, 2012 at 7:12pm ·**

Personal life

Donald Marshall on: his age
3SG1: How old are you, Donald?

DM: I am 36 now... I was about 23 when I posed for that oil painting *as a REM driven duplicate clone* at the cloning center. The painting was later displayed on the cover of the Megadeth Album titled "The World Needs a Hero" (2001) [the album was released 3 years later in 2001 when I was about 26]... I haven't aged much since... thankfully. **May 9, 2012 at 9:27pm**

March 25th 2012

Donald Marshall uploads pictures of himself (real body) to his Facebook timeline
DM: These are new pictures of me by BlackBerry.

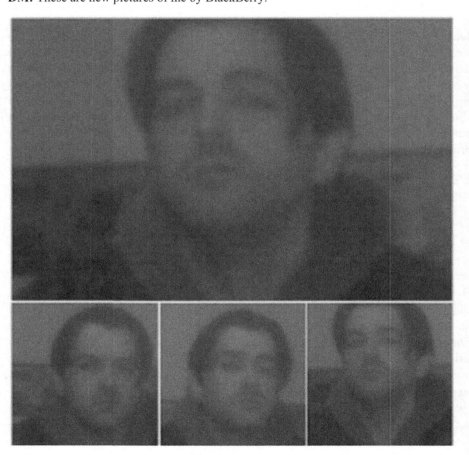

3SG1: Did you take these pictures?

DM: No. A buddy of mine did. I will be making video of me. It will be clear. I will do it soon and I will post it [on Facebook]. **May 8, 2012 at 6:46pm**

3SG2: Donald, are your pictures up yet?

DM: Yes. The pictures are in my profile, the privacy is set to "Public" so you should be able to see the pictures, like everyone else can. **April 25, 2012 at 4:14pm**

May 10th 2012

Donald Marshall's friend posts a clearer picture of Donald Marshall (real body)

3SG1: I cleaned up one of your photos so people could see it better.

May 16th 2012

Donald Marshall's girlfriend leaves him

DM: UPDATE: SO my live-in girlfriend [girlfriend who was living with me] just left me unexpectedly! I do not know where she went; she is TERRIFIED that we are going to be shot by an NWO (New World Order) death squad. I cannot blame her for leaving, really. Keep helping me my friends. I hope she is somewhere safe.

3SG1: I can understand her fear, Donny.

3SG2: If you ever feel lonely Donald, just remember: there are 245 people (this current moment) that love and support you.

DM: This is the last post I will make today before I make the longer video tonight. 245 is the number of people on my Facebook friends list. There are thousands of people watching me... Most people watching are scared to be on my friends list; therefore I made privacy settings "Public" so that everyone who is on Facebook, and not necessarily on my Facebook friends list can see the posts I make. Even though the NWO / Illuminati monitor me closely and see every post I receive or make... ever since videos about me containing information about the Illuminati's REM driven cloning subculture have been uploaded to YouTube there are many, many concerned people mailing me more each day. The disclosure of the Illuminati and their REM driven cloning subculture is going well and get's bigger every day. **May 19, 2012 at 6:19pm**

Song Making

Why the Illuminati members and musicians want Donald Marshall to make songs for them

3SG1: Donald, why would people want you to write their lyrics?

DM: I've made songs at the cloning center since I was a child at age 5. The Illuminati grew multiple duplicate clones of me when I went to the doctor's to have my foreskin removed at age 4. Five months later they had grown multiple duplicate clones of me and were transferring my consciousness from my original body to my duplicate *REM driven* clone whenever I entered REM sleep. Initially, the Illuminati brought me there *(through the process of consciousness transfer, and activated my consciousness in duplicate REM driven clone of me)* to be used as a paedophile victim, what they term "A Diddle Kid". I said as a child *REM driven* clone "I don't want to get gross with old people!" And they said "Well can you do anything else? Can you sing or dance?" So I made a song. A Really good song; the first one I made was titled "Lady" later performed by Kenny Rogers (Robin Francis 2008). I sang it to Queen Elizabeth II *as a REM driven clone* as a child *REM driven* clone at the cloning center. The Illuminati members, *as REM driven clone versions of themselves*, then deactivated my *REM driven* clone, and let me go for the night. But then, they transferred my consciousness again to my *REM driven* clone a few nights later when I went to sleep, and I made another good song, then they would deactivate my *REM driven* clone and let me go for the night. The songs that I was making as a *REM driven* clone when I was a child, turned out to be top 10 hits. All of them; and it was weird how I could just freestyle a song out of thin air. When they realised I had a gift for song making this is when they started transferring my consciousness to my *REM driven* clone whenever I slept and brought me to the cloning centers *(through the process of consciousness transfer from the original's body to the duplicate REM driven clone)* regularly, so that Tina Turner and Bryan Adams, Madonna, and Whitney Houston etc. could have songs to sing. The Illuminati said "I had the gift of melody to get a song stuck in someone's head"... Then, the torture of my *REM driven* clones began after I started to have trouble free-styling songs or making songs with the technology they have at the cloning centers (Mind-voice technology; MK Ultra technology). Now the Illuminati THINK I have some kind of religious significance; or they are playing it that way to make their empty existence mean something. The Illuminati have said I am part of their religion (a **FAKE** religion); and it keeps celebrities attending the cloning centers *as REM driven clone versions of themselves*. This is what the political and average people there who attend the cloning centers *as their REM driven clone versions* want.... They want a draw to lure the celebrities to hang with them *as REM driven clones* at the cloning center... **April 5, 2012 at 3:14pm**

Donald Marshall on: Coldplay

3SG1: How many songs did you write for Coldplay? What do you mean they are b******s? How so?

DM: OK, I don't like to mention songs because I did so many songs it is hard to fathom. But I did almost all the Coldplay songs [either by free-styling them or using the technologies they have at the cloning centers –Mind-voice technology; MK Ultra technology]. I basically am Coldplay. <u>July 2, 2012 at 11:13am</u>

3SG1: No way. Coldplay?! What are they like? They seem nice but you say they aren't. You wrote almost all of their songs... But did they put their own music to it? It is unfathomable. Thanks for answering.

Donald Marshall on: Coldplay and Chris Martin

DM: Coldplay? I have only met the lead singer Chris Martin, *as REM driven clones of ourselves* at the cloning center, and the band Coldplay does not make anything music wise. *As a REM driven clone at the cloning center* I had to make the melody, guitar, bass, drums, and lyrics of their songs [the melody, guitar, bass, and drums etc was achieved through Mind-voice technology or MK Ultra technology]... Coldplay later performs the music I made *(as a REM driven clone at the cloning center)*. Coldplay had no creative input in the music they play. The Illuminati did **NOT** allow Coldplay to have any creative input in the music which they play. Furthermore, when I talked to Chris Martin *as REM driven clones* at the cloning center, Chris Martin treated me as a dog slave beneath him: "Hurry up and spit out my next song or things will get ugly" –was the type of interaction we had. <u>July 2, 2012 at 11:43am</u>

Donald Marshall on: Coldplay and Fiona Apple

3SG1: That is F****D [that Chris Martin treated you that way as a REM driven clone]. What about Fiona Apple [did you make her songs too]?

DM: Fiona Apple sings songs I made at the cloning center *as a REM driven clone version of myself.* Fiona Apple is a weirdo. <u>July 2, 2012 at 12:03pm</u>

3SG1: ALL of them [Fiona Apple's] are your songs?

DM: Not all of Fiona Apple's songs were made by me *as a REM driven clone at the cloning center*. But nearly all of Coldplay's songs which they perform were made by me at the cloning center *as a REM driven clone*. Nearly all of Coldplay's songs were made by me *as a REM driven clone*, except for example, two non-famous songs. <u>July 2, 2012 at 12:14pm</u>

3SG1: How many of Fiona Apple's songs did you make? So basically you're saying no one has any talent or is capable of writing their music? I know none of the cheap pop stars write their own songs but Fiona Apple plays the piano, as does Coldplay; they are talented. I did not mean for that to sound nasty. How is Fiona a weirdo? What does she do [as a REM driven clone at the cloning centers]? I can't imagine Fiona Apple would cope there [as a REM driven clone at the cloning centers] nor can I imagine how Winona Ryder would cope *as a REM driven clone at the cloning centers.*

DM: So you are saying just because Coldplay and Fiona Apple play piano they're talented? Fiona is a filthy gutter tramp *as a REM driven clone at the cloning center* OR Fiona Apple **was** in the past; and Fiona Apple always tried to act evil *as a REM driven clone* at the cloning centers whenever the opportunity presented. Winona Ryder did not act evil *as a REM driven clone* at the cloning centers. Fiona Apple is rotten. Furthermore, the way was paved for Coldplay by influential parents within cloning circles... **July 2, 2012 at 12:22pm**

"Drive By" made by Donald Marshall performed by Train

DM: OH listen: a couple of months ago while at the cloning center *as a REM driven clone* the Illuminati members made me make a song while I was drugged as a *REM driven* clone version of myself. It is a new song out now: "On the other side of a street I knew, stood a girl that looked like you" called "Drive by" performed by "Train" (TrainVEVO 2012)... but you will like this: originally the words were: " ON THE UPSIDE OF A DOWNWARD SPIRAL... MY DOCUMENT WENT VIRAL!" The Illuminati made me change that part of the song *(as a REM driven clone, at the cloning center)* to "**my love** for you went viral..." – and then the Illuminati members got mad because they said it sounds like the song is now talking about an STD [Sexually Transmitted Disease]... The Illuminati fear the letter though guys... and every time someone new reads the letter (Donald Marshall Proboards 2012) (as well as my other disclosure documents) I become one step closer to salvation. Continue to spread the truth about the Illuminati's REM driven cloning subculture, guys. This will work. It **HAS** to. **April 12, 2012 at 6:38pm**

3SG1: I just heard that song you mentioned performed by "Train" on the Rachel Ray Show ... it's called "Drive By"

DM: I made it *as a REM driven clone* at the cloning center... "Drive by"... "Upward twist to a downward spiral, MY DOCUMENT WENT VIRAL..." All the *REM driven* clones sitting in the stands at the cloning center started shifting in their seats and looking at each other worried when I said that... I have made so many songs at the cloning center *as a REM driven clone* it is unfathomable... **April 17, 2012 at 8:48pm**

"Say It Right" made by Donald Marshall performed by Nelly Furtado and Timberland

3SG1: If people still do not believe [your testimonies regarding REM driven cloning], you can always post one of your songs you wrote at your own time [as a REM driven clone at the cloning centers], but one that no one can find the lyrics to on Google. That'd be enough proof. Not many people can write songs, and especially not hit songs.

DM: Writing the lyrics to one of the songs I made at the cloning center *as a REM driven clone* which currently cannot be found on Google will not prove anything. People will just say "I got lucky"... or something. Having said that, I try to put little hints into almost all of the songs I made *as a REM driven clone version of myself* at the cloning center. For example in the song performed by Nelly Furtado and Timberland "Say It Right" (NellyFurtadoVEVO 2009), I said while singing Nelly's part "(((Space is cloning)))" (which can be heard at 3:08 min of the song; NellyFurtadoVEVO 2009). The Illuminati members wanted me to change that part of the song to something else but I said *(as a REM driven clone at the cloning center)* "Who cares. Just make it like that". That line does not make sense in the song... but that is exactly what Nelly Furtado says.

DM: I would just like to make a song saying: **"Help me. I'm cloned and getting hurt"** but the Illuminati do not allow that. I need polygraph tests from independent, unbiased testers. Now I realise that nobody is going to be able to say "OK Queen Elizabeth II –lie detector test time; or Brad Pitt –lie detector test time", of course, BUT the independent unbiased polygraph testers can test me, and ground level members like my mother and step father and his brothers and other ground level members. The Illuminati fear that... **April 22, 2012 at 6:26pm**

Donald Marshall on: The Prodigy

3SG1: Donald, have you made songs for The Prodigy?

DM: The Prodigy? I have MADE songs for The Prodigy *as a REM driven clone* at the cloning center. I would freestyle the songs from start to finish. The lead singer of The Prodigy (Keith Flint) knows all about me and REM driven cloning. Keith Flint is a low level Illuminati member. I made "Firestarter" (The Prodigy 2008b) for The Prodigy and another big song "Breathe" (The Prodigy 2008a) for The Prodigy *as a REM driven clone* at the cloning center. I have made so many songs as a REM driven clone at the cloning center it is off the scale. The Illuminati tell me I have made more songs; super-hit songs too, nearly every time; more than anyone on earth ever; even as far back as to biblical times... that is why I am not dead yet... However, the Illuminati want me to stop mailing about them, and gradually get me back to making songs *as a REM driven clone* at the cloning center for their celebrity friends who attend the cloning centers *as REM driven clone versions of themselves.* **April 24, 2012 at 7:59pm**

"Is Anybody Out There?" made by Donald Marshall performed by K'NAAN ft Nelly Furtado

3SG1: Donald, can you possibly make a song about something we can relate to, via this information? Something which will make us, think: "Donald Marshall wrote this song".

DM: Um... seriously... there are thousands of songs available which reference this information [the Illuminati's REM driven cloning subculture], and there are many songs which contain hints to this information; what do you think you have been listening to...? But OK...Here is a song which I sang recently at the cloning centers *as a REM driven clone* which has just been released, and it is performed by K'NAAN featuring Nelly Furtado titled "Is Anybody Out There?" (KnaanVEVO 2012) When I sang "Is Anybody Out There?" (KnaanVEVO 2012) *as a REM driven clone* at the cloning center, I did not think the Illuminati would allow this song to be released. Nevertheless, there is a woman on a website who is helping me spread the information, and at the time she insisted that we should have a banner for this information; and I said OK the Illuminati allowed me to say in the rap part of the song [K'NAAN's part, verse 4] "There goes Nina showing off her banner, shaking up the crown make the boys go bananas" and the lyrics is **NOT**: "crowd" NOR "There goes **Hannah** showing off her banner, **rocking** that crown, make them boys go bananas" as you would find on the lyric sheet (AZLyrics 2012). The words have been changed; however as a *REM driven* clone at the cloning center when I sang "Is Anybody Out There?" (KnaanVEVO 2012) I said "Nina", "shaking" and "crown".

Donald Marshall on: Nickelback

DM: Furthermore, and I am not bragging; however, *as a REM driven clone at the cloning center*, I was **forced** to make all the songs Nickelback have performed; I even had to name the band *when I was a REM driven clone at the cloning center*. All of the songs which Nickelback have performed and are well known for, I was forced as a *REM driven* clone at the cloning center to produce for Nickelback, all except Nickelback's latest song which has just been released. Nickelback's latest song was shown to me at the cloning center recently when I was *a REM driven clone version of myself* at the cloning center. The song is called "This Means War" (Roadrunner Records 2012). It is Nickelback's latest song and it is supposedly about me, as the Illuminati *REM driven clones* have said. It is about how angry the Illuminati is with me; and it is even mentioned in the song "This Means War" (Roadrunner Records 2012)   "The only thing to save, is the banner that you wave, to be wrapped around your grave"; "You've gone too farrrrrrr"; "Who do you think you are?" Just look it up (Roadrunner Records 2012).

Donald Marshall on: *"Is Anybody Out There?"*; *"This Means War"*; and *"Good Feeling"*

DM: I only made a few songs as a *REM driven* clone recently because the Illuminati *REM driven clones* said to me, as a *REM driven* clone at the cloning center, "If I could think up a song, I could leave the cloning center unharmed that night", so I did. Look up those two songs: "Is Anybody Out There?" performed by K'NAAN featuring Nelly Furtado (KnaanVEVO 2012) and "This Means War" by Nickelback (Roadrunner Records 2012). Furthermore, look up the song "Good Feeling" performed by "Flo Rida" (Flo Rida 2011) –it is about me, and this situation. That song has all kinds of references, and I have provided the lyrics here [in this document, on the next page] as I sang them as a REM driven clone at the cloning center –and you can compare what the words have been changed to (AZLyrics 2011b). The song "Good Feeling" (Flo Rida 2011) is filled with many references; I include references whenever I make songs as *a REM driven clone* at the cloning center, and the Illuminati *REM driven clones* (sometimes) just let me. **April 30, 2012 at 4:39am ·**

Yes I can, y'all better leave I'll be down with this plan
Pull me, grab me, crabs in a bucket can't have me
I'll be the President one day, January 1st
Hope you like that gossip
Like you're the one thinking what god sip dot com
Now I've got a verb for your tongue
How many Rolling Stones do you want?
Yeh I gotta brand new feeling for getting this done
Woke up on the side of the bed like I won
Heart beating out of my chest, and it's on
G5 feeling, US to Taiwan
Now who can say that, I need a playback
Momma always knew, I was a needle in a hay stack
I'm a Bali-boy, plus I'm laid back
I got a feeling it's a wrap A-SAP

The mountain top, walk on water
I've got power, feel so raw you
One second, imma strike all you
Diamond, platinum, no more for you
Got adrenaline, never giving in
Giving up's not an option, gotta get it in
Greatness, I've got the heart of 20 men
No deal, go to sleep when the lights dim
That flow that sparks that crowd
You're looking at "The King", got his jaws groomed now
Stones and my hammer, can't slow me down
A hundred miles running from you bitches now
Straight game face, it's game day
See me running through the crowd full of mêlée
No quick plays, I'm Bill Gates
Take your DREAMS to understand me

Donald Marshall on: Maroon 5 and Adam Levine

3SG1: What about Adam Levine from Maroon 5, is he involved [in REM driven cloning]?

DM: As a _REM driven_ clone version of myself at the cloning center, I made every single song Maroon 5 ever recorded. Adam Levine attends the cloning center as _a REM driven clone version of himself_, and Adam Levine knows ALL about me, REM driven cloning and everything I have said. Adam Levine sits in the stands at the cloning center _as a REM driven clone of himself_, and Adam Levine will see this post and he will be very annoyed that I mentioned his name. As a _REM driven_ clone version of myself, I made the song "Misery" (Maroon5VEVO 2010) at the cloning center, and the song "Misery" was later performed by Maroon 5 (Maroon5VEVO 2010). The song "Misery" (Maroon5VEVO 2010) is about my time spent the cloning center as a _REM driven_ clone and how I am going to get Queen Elizabeth II back... word for word.... I am going to get all the Illuminati _REM driven clones_ back... me... all of them... Adam Levine is scum... **May 10, 2012 at 3:36pm ·**

"Titanium" made by Donald Marshall performed by David Guetta ft Sia

DM: I've come to McDonald's to use their Wi-Fi and there is a song being played right now called "Titanium" performed by David Guetta featuring Sia (David Guetta 2011). As a _REM driven_ clone version of myself at the cloning center I sang the song "Titanium" (David Guetta 2011) to Prime Minster Stephen Harper who was also a _REM driven_ clone version of himself at the cloning center. As a _REM driven_ clone version of himself at the cloning center, Prime Minister Stephen Harper has shot my _REM driven_ clones a few times [listen to the song "Titanium" and you can hear "being shot" referenced many times; also look up the song lyrics (AZLyrics 2011a)]. I do not like the song "Titanium" (David Guetta 2011). **May 15, 2012 at 2:02am**

Donald Marshall on: Flo Rida's self-made song "Whistle"

DM: Flo Rida just made his first song, all by himself titled "Whistle" (The Live Room powered by Warner Music 2012). The song has a repetitive chorus "Can you blow my whistle baby, whistle baby" etc. Flo Rida is making fun of me... As a _REM driven_ clone version of myself at the cloning center, I made all of the previous songs Flo Rida later performed prior to his new song "Whistle" (The Live Room powered by Warner Music 2012). As you have probably guessed, the new Flo Rida song, "Whistle" is about me; whistle blowing... (The Live Room powered by Warner Music 2012) **May 15, 2012 at 2:02am ·**

Donald Marshall explains the lyrics to the song "Good Feeling" performed by Flo Rida

DM: I HAVE something for you guys to look at, performed by a rapper named Flo Rida. As a *REM driven* clone version of myself, activated unwillingly at the cloning center, I made almost all of the songs Flo Rida later performed when I was activated as a *REM driven* clone at the cloning center. You should listen to his recent song called "Good Feeling" (Flo Rida 2011); I made this song recently at the cloning center when I was unwillingly activated as a *REM driven* clone version of myself... I left many clues in the songs where I could... Remember the religious significance the Illuminati members believe I have? Well listen to the rap parts of the song which goes as follows (Flo Rida 2011):

Donald Marshall explains: "Good Feeling" lyrics performed by Flo Rida

Yes I can, y'all better leave I'll be down with this plan
Pull me, grab me, crabs in a bucket can't have me
I'll be the President one day, January 1st
Hope you like that gossip
Like you're the one thinking what god sip dot com
Now I've got a verb for your tongue
How many Rolling Stones do you want?

[The lyric directly above is, rhyming space filler. Listen]

Yeh I gotta brand new feeling for getting this done
Woke up on the side of the bed like I won
Heart beating out of my chest, and it's on
G5 feeling, US to Taiwan
Now who can say that, I need a playback
Momma always knew, I was a needle in a hay stack
I'm a Bali-boy, plus I'm laid back
I got a feeling it's a wrap A-SAP

[The second verse below is filled with even more references]

The mountain top, walk on water
I've got power, feel so raw you
One second, imma strike all you
Diamond, platinum, no more for you

[the lyrics directly above is about how I will NOT be making diamond and platinum records for the Illuminati anymore. Listen]

Got adrenaline, never giving in
Giving up's not an option, gotta get it in

[the lyrics directly above is about how I have to keep mailing and informing the world about human cloning and the Illuminati's REM driven cloning subculture].

Greatness, I've got the heart of 20 men
No deal, go to sleep when the lights dim
That flow that sparks that crowd
You're looking at "The King", got his jaws groomed now
Stones and my hammer, can't slow me down
A hundred miles running from you bitches now
Straight game face, it's game day
See me running through the crowd full of mêlée
No quick plays, I'm Bill Gates
Take your DREAMS to understand me

[*As REM driven clone versions of ourselves at the cloning center*, Flo Rida said *as a REM driven clone version of himself*, that he changed "dreams" to "genius"].

Donald Marshall on: "Good Feeling" and "Whistle"

DM: Now Flo Rida has made his first song without me and Flo Rida is making fun of me with his first independent song. The song is called "Whistle" by Flo Rida (The Live Room powered by Warner Music 2012). There are many more songs with references to this information [the Illuminati's REM driven cloning subculture] such as the two songs I have motioned above "Good Feeling" (Flo Rida 2011) and "Whistle" (The Live Room powered by Warner Music 2012).

3SG1: I saw Flo Rida sing "Whistle" (Flo Rida 2011) on TV and I did notice that some of the words to the song seemed symbolic!

"Shut It Down" made by Donald Marshall performed by Pitbull ft. Akon

DM: Listen to the song "Shut It Down" performed by Pitbull and Akon (PitbullVEVO 2009). I made this song *as a REM driven clone of myself* at the cloning center. Jewish people who attend the cloning center *as REM driven clones of themselves*, wanted me, *as a REM driven clone of myself*, to say the name of the Jewish god YAHWEH in the song "Shut It Down" (PitbullVEVO 2009).... However, it is against their religion to speak the name with a human voice... SO... listen to the song and you will hear Pitbull say "now watch me, now watch me, now watch me shut this thing down"... and a robotic voice says "YAH.WEH.....YAH.WEH..." It is absolutely obvious (PitbullVEVO 2009). You can hear this clearly in the song, but you will not find it on the lyric sheet (MetroLyrics 2009). There are many references such as this, regarding references which relate to the Illuminati's REM driven cloning subculture. Tomorrow, I will be telling everyone about area 51 and the crashed flying saucer.

"Raspberry Beret" made by Donald Marshall performed by Prince about Muammar Gaddafi

3SG1: I am curious as to why the YouTube account with Stevey's [Steven Joseph Christopher's] arrest video (uploaded 3 years ago) is called "Raspberryberrett05" while "Raspberry Beret" is the song you [Donald Marshall] claim to have wrote for Prince in a testimony to Stevey [Steven Joseph Christopher] a mere week ago?

3SG2: Donald Marshall said he wrote "Raspberry Beret"?

3SG1: You would have known that [3SG2] if you were able to persevere through the vast spelling and grammatical errors, typos in him [Donald Marshall] and "Stevey the Saviour's" [Steven Joseph Christopher's] long winded Facebook conversation full of contradictions.

DM: Yes, "Raspberry Beret" (Peterjochu 2012; LyricsFreak 2016) was written by me as a *REM driven* clone child at the cloning center [when I was about ten years old] about Muammar Gaddafi for Prince [to sing] (Peterjochu 2012; LyricsFreak 2016). It is unknown to me why Stevie's [Steven Joseph Christopher's] video was called "Raspberryberrett05" –it is a coincidence. I never knew Steven Joseph Christopher until approximately one month ago [through Facebook]. He is whacked [crazy]. **May 18, 2012 at 5:04pm ·**

3SG1: His [Steven Joseph Christopher's] response: "Yea, I'm familiar with that song". The god-damned YouTube account is called "Raspberryberrett05" and that's all he could say in response to this incredible coincidence? You [Donald Marshall] are absolutely right he [Steven Joseph Christopher] is whacked [crazy]. He [Steven Joseph Christopher] claims to be Jesus Christ and seems to possess the faculties of someone who... well, is NOT Jesus Christ?

DM: I know. I had to disassociate myself with Steven [Joseph Christopher]. Steven Joseph Christopher was counterproductive and turned negative when I said he is not God or Jesus... Steven Joseph Christopher is just a nutter [crazy]...

DM: I had no way of knowing Steven Joseph Christopher's YouTube account was called "Raspberryberrett05" because I did not know Steven Joseph Christopher three years ago [in real life or as REM driven clones at the cloning center; nor did I know Steven Joseph Christopher during the time which he made that YouTube account]. I've only known Steven Joseph Christopher through Facebook, and met him on Facebook a month ago on Facebook. **May 18, 2012 at 5:15pm ·**

"Cut's like a knife" made by Donald Marshall performed by Bryan Adams

3SG1: Donald, I was able to contact Bryan Adams' guitar player [Keith Scott] and asked if he or Bryan Adams has ever heard of you. He said no. Then I forwarded your letter [about human cloning and the Illuminati's REM driven cloning subculture] to him and he [Bryan Adams' guitar player] responded with a not so nice character assassination about you.

Donald Marshall on: Bryan Adams

DM: *Laughter*. Bryan Adams' guitar player [Keith Scott] might not even know about the Illuminati's REM driven cloning subculture or about me, himself. *As a REM driven clone version of myself*, I only dealt with Bryan Adams *as a REM driven clone version of himself*, as well as, whoever claims they wrote the songs with Bryan Adams' *as a REM driven clone version of themselves* at the cloning center. Bryan Adams knows about the Illuminati REM driven cloning subculture because we have spoken face to face as *REM driven* clone versions of ourselves at the cloning center. Bryan Adams also knows who I am. As a *REM driven* clone version of myself at the cloning center, I made all of the songs Bryan Adams performed since he sang "Cuts like a knife" (Bryan Adams 2008). You cannot lie on a lie detector guys... [And this will be proven clearly to everyone soon]. This is going to be awesome! **May 18, 2012 at 5:43pm ·**

Donald Marshall on: Bryan Adams' involvement with REM driven cloning

3SG1: He [Keith Scott] asked Bryan [Adams] if Bryan [Adams] had heard of you and Bryan said "No".

DM: *Uncontrollable laughter*... Well I expected Bryan Adams to say (*sarcasm*)... "Yes. I know Donald Marshall. We grew duplicate clones of him when he was a child, and we would transfer his consciousness whenever the real him went to sleep and reached REM sleep, to his *REM driven* clone at the cloning center, and the best part was we suppressed his memory so that when he woke up from sleep he wouldn't remember his time spent at the cloning center as a *REM driven* clone. So we cloned Donny into the cloning center and if you threatened Donny with being stabbed as a *REM driven* clone version of himself at the cloning center, Donny would make an amazing song for you... but then Donny run out of ideas for songs so we stabbed him as a *REM driven* clone kid in his sleep... and to keep himself from getting stabbed as a *REM driven* clone kid in his sleep, Donny made an amazing song again... but then it got worse... we just stabbed Donny as a *REM driven* clone of himself at the cloning center for fun anyway because we were jealous of his unique talent [of being able to make amazing songs by free-styling songs and sometimes with the use of the highly advanced technologies that we have at the cloning center, but do not tell the public about]... then everyone you could think of, wanted a song from Donny whenever he was activated as a *REM driven* clone version of himself at the cloning center...

DM: Hey everyone was doing it... so why not me too [Bryan Adams]" (*end sarcasm*). No, none of the people I have dealt with as *REM driven* clone versions of themselves at the cloning center are going to say that... They will in the future though... and not in the distant future... **May 18, 2012 at 6:09pm**

Technologies

May 17th 2012

Area 51 and Flying Saucers

DM: OK! I promised you Unidentified Flying Object (UFO) Area 51 information and I shall deliver. Flying saucers are American made [man made]. The Americans made a technology called "matter displacement". "Matter displacement" could be mistaken for 'anti-gravity' but I was told *when I was activated as a REM driven clone version of myself* by the Illuminati REM *driven clones* that it is not 'anti gravity' but rather matter displacement technology. This matter displacement technology has also been demonstrated on a documentary on TV: three beams of matter displacement was demonstrated; furthermore the flying saucer was unstable and I do not even know how the pilot managed to survive the g-forces, but anyway, in a flying saucer the top and bottom spin alternately to make a gyro effect; it is similar to spinning a bicycle tyre horizontally and then trying to turn the bicycle tyre vertically; it is a difficult feat to achieve because the centrifugal force keeps the flying saucer more stable... then two beams stabilise the flying saucer and a third beam pushes the saucer backwards... However, controlling the movement of a flying saucer is very erratic. Flying saucers were first tested at Area 51, but these saucers were too unstable and could have zipped off in any direction and land unexpectedly in the nearest town. Therefore, in order to conceal their research, the Americans put Egyptian hieroglyphics on their saucers to systematically deceive people and hide the truth if ever the American's research into flying saucers and matter displacement technology was to be discovered. The Americans did not want Russians or any nation for that matter to know that Americans were in the process of researching flying saucers and matter displacement technology... Furthermore, can you recall the material which was found that was claimed to be 'extraterrestrial'? Well this material was actually "mylar". It is now public knowledge that mylar material exists, however, the official account states that we HAVE mylar material now, but we did not have mylar material at the time of the UFO flying saucer crash. Well yes, the Americans did have mylar material as far back as the early 1950s; the Americans just did not tell the public anything about mylar material. Furthermore, during the American's research into flying saucer technology and matter displacement technology, the Americans realised that flying saucers were useless for war; bullets go straight through flying saucers; and the flying saucers required a lot of power, and a lot of force, even for a short flight.

DM: Moreover, during the time of the American's research into flying saucer technology (late 1940s) the Americans / Illuminati had never met any grey aliens... or any extraterrestrials yet. *As a REM driven clone version of myself at the cloning center*, I **begged** the Illuminati *REM driven clones* to tell me everything they knew about grey aliens and extraterrestrials. I cried many times as a *REM driven* clone child at the cloning center, because I was a very curious *REM driven* clone child and wanted to know any truth there is to know about grey aliens or extraterrestrials. The Illuminati *REM driven clones* told me as a *REM driven* clone version of myself at the cloning center that people watch the documentary about flying saucers and disregard it as "false" because people WANT to believe in aliens and HAVE something to talk about...

The documentary on flying saucers, explains the technology of flying saucers in great detail, and the documentary concludes that flying saucers are in fact useless. The general public perception is that the documentary on flying saucers is just an attempt by the government to 'cover up' for aliens... but really it is **not** an attempt of a cover up... flying saucers are legitimately failed technology. There is research into many high advances in technology which is tested at Area 51 and there is supposedly a cloning center underground at Area 51. Area 51 looks like the Stargate base [Stargate Command (SGC) Base] depicted on TV. As a *REM driven* clone version of myself, I have only been to Area 51 once as a *REM driven clone*, and I have never seen the outside of Area 51, *as a REM driven clone version of myself.*

Furthermore, the matter displacement technology will give a person cancer if the matter displacement technology goes over a person's body; matter displacement technology is also very dangerous. Matter displacement technology involves magnets fuelled by electricity. A person died while working on the invention of matter displacement technology; two magnets became attracted to each other which sparked an explosion and the magnets scattered into shrapnel... I have knowledge of many highly advanced technologies which currently exist to tell everyone about... this includes MK Ultra mind control technology... Yes, MK Ultra mind control technology does exist and I will tell you how it is done; it involves clones. To summarise: unfortunately there are no grey aliens... -that is movie stuff... but if you were to ask about reptilians on the other hand...? Well, reptilians are a story for another day...

3SG1: There are more than fifty types of grey aliens. Are you crazy? Grey aliens are far better documented than reptilians. I am not sure how anybody cannot describe this [the information which Donald Marshall has presented] as scaremongering... has any actual proof surfaced [regarding the Illuminati's REM driven cloning subculture] other than that of Tila Tequila?

DM: There are no grey aliens... 3SG1 you are just wrong, dude. I **begged** the Illuminati *REM driven clones* when I was a child *REM driven* clone at the cloning center to tell me everything about grey aliens... The Illuminati members *as REM driven clone versions of themselves* have never met grey aliens. Tila Tequila has to tread lightly now. The Illuminati members, *as REM driven clone versions of themselves*, at the cloning center, told Tila Tequila *when she was a REM driven clone of herself* that: "If she mentions "clones" there will be no second chance and she will have her brain swell till she dies, remotely!" They have given Tila Tequila a brain aneurysm before, so she is skirting on the edge. Tila Tequila is telling the world about the Illuminati's REM driven cloning subculture vaguely, and how human cloning / REM driven cloning involves slavery...

DM: Tila Tequila is just not allowed to say "clone" or "replicated bodies" or anything which hints at human cloning... Tila Tequila wants to leave the Illuminati REM driven cloning subculture permanently. The Illuminati members probably offered Tila Tequila another TV show in exchange to keep her quiet... I have spoken to Tila Tequila many times face to face as *REM driven* clones at the cloning center... and I wish she would join me and this cause. Tila Tequila is scared though... I am scared too... but I have no choice but to speak out on the matter... If I fail, the Illuminati members will become more confident that nobody will ever catch them and they will renew torturing me as a *REM driven* clone version of myself at the cloning center, badly, as punishment and as an example. I have no choice but to continue informing the world about the Illuminati's REM driven cloning subculture... soon the floodgates open. **May 18, 2012 at 5:12pm**

Contact Information

Facebook: https://www.facebook.com/donald.marshall.148

Press Ctrl+Click (hold "Ctrl" on your keyboard and left "Click" with your mouse, on the image to your right to be taken to my Facebook page).

My Facebook timeline starts from March 2012. All posts are "Public" and therefore newcomers should start reading from March 2012, in order to fully understand the Illuminati's REM driven cloning subculture and more. You may start reading my Facebook public timeline from May 18th 2012, ONCE you have finished reading each document listed as "Volume 1" in the series.

Donald Marshall Proboards (Forum):
http://donaldmarshall.proboards.com/board/1/general-board

There is a "search" function on Proboards, and you can use this function to search for and read all the disclosures I have made regarding REM driven clones, the people involved and more. I understand that it is human nature to want to know which people have been to the cloning centre as REM driven clones; therefore, use the "search" function to read about any public figure which I have already covered that you have an inkling about. You can also post anonymously on Proboards and Celine and other Administrators will transfer your question onto Facebook, which I'll answer.

Donald Marshall Revolution: http://donaldmarshallrevolution.com/
Donald Marshall Revolution details a brief overview of the Illuminati's REM driven cloning subculture; it also gives the viewer the most significant information relating to my disclosures in a small and easily understood style.

Twitter: https://twitter.com/dmarshalltruth
Follow me on twitter and help share spread the information regarding the Illuminati and their REM driven cloning subculture.

Email: donny865@hotmail.com

I currently have over 35,000 unread emails in my hotmail inbox, and counting at the address above. I cannot respond to all of these messages, unfortunately, at this present stage of events. It is better to contact me through Facebook and private message me this way. You can also contact Celine on Facebook, or leave a message with Celine on the forum (Donald Marshall Proboards) and she will forward your message to me. I really appreciate everyone's efforts and well wishes.

Interviews

Readers can listen to the radio interviews I have done. Listen for consistency; particular
anything which you do not hear me, pronounce clearly for the first time; the best thing to
is to pause the recording at that particular point and replay it. You should also research th
statements you do not understand. Sometimes reading helps comprehension a lot faster.

One of the main reasons you should pause and replay the recordings is because: the truth h
been kept hidden for so long that a lot of what I discuss in my interviews are beyond mo
people's current world view; so at some points I may speak too fast for you; my audio
microphone may not be so clear so you may miss what I say etc. Others have also comment
on the fact that they pretended 'as if': I was someone from the distant future sent back in tin
(I am **NOT**); to give important information to the world about highly advanced technolog
which currently exist but are hidden and secret and being used against the populace. Und
such a premise these people rationalised that they would not understand the informatic
which was being presented to them straight away, and they would have to be patient in ord
to grasp certain concepts, technical speak, and the highly advanced technologies et
BEFORE they can grasp the **SERIOUSNESS** of the information presented.

Furthermore, a friend has told me that when he first watched the Vinny Eastwood intervie
he did not hear me say the word "scars" (When Vinny asked: 'How do I know I'm the re
me?') although he replayed that particular point in the video 8 times. Everything was ju
beyond his current comprehension, at the time. No matter how many times he replayed th
part he really could not hear me say the word "scars" –so he let that part go, and played th
rest of the interview, pausing, and replaying points which he did not understand, especially
comprehend whether I was talking about my original body or my REM driven clone duplica
body. He also listened to all my interviews for consistency, to note any 'slip ups', or any pa
of my testimonies which do not 'add up'. He would listen to all my interviews, pausing a
replaying parts he did not understand and he would reserve his judgements until he fo
everything I was saying was for example as ordinary as: 'I woke up today, brushed my tee
and took the dog for a walk'. He was also patient to realise the truth. After listening to n
interviews he would just let it 'sink in'. A week later he would come back and listen to th
same interviews, to test whether his comprehension on the topics I discuss has improved, a
whether he can understand what I am saying without having to pause and repeat at certa
points in my interview; and soon enough he could now hear me say "scars" at that particul
point of the Vinny Eastwood interview. He had reached the point where all topics I discu
sounded to him like I'm saying everyday common place stuff that people have heard, such a
'I woke up today, brushed my teeth, and took the dog for a walk'. For anyone who ma
struggle to understand the topics I discuss: I strongly recommend you take the abo
approach as my friend did; soon enough, you too will realise the real truth of the world li
he has: REM driven cloning, kept secret and used for sinister purposes.

I cannot say the following is true for everybody, however, an unproductive venture
complete newcomer can do is to listen to my interviews first time, all the way throug
without pausing or replaying parts which they do not fully understand; if you do this, and
there is just a single part of my interviews which does not make sense to you; this w
interfere with your understanding of the entire interview.

Radio Presenters –Contact Donald Marshall

Any Radio Presenters who sincerely want to contact me for radio interviews on their show is welcome to do this. Please contact me through Proboards by leaving a message for me to contact you.

Professionals who understand "Consciousness Transfer" –Contact Donald Marshall

Neuroscientists, engineers or professionals who understand how consciousness transfer works, and can provide me with a detailed methodology of how to block the consciousness transfer to my REM driven clone; please message me on Proboards, and this will be greatly appreciated.

Other Sources Corroborating Donald Marshall

Press Ctrl+Click (on the images below to be directed to each source)

Astral 7ight Blogspot
http://astral7ight.blogspot.co.uk/

Astral 7ight has compiled Donald Marshall's disclosures regarding the Illuminati's *REM driven human* cloning subculture extensively. Astral 7ight also details his experiences as a victim of *REM driven* human cloning, and as a consequence, Astral 7ight corroborates Donald Marshall's exposure of the Illuminati's *REM driven human* cloning subculture as humanity's current reality.

Donald Marshall Books:
https://drive.google.com/folderview?id=0B6uNZqRUN8ceQnRRaGl1VEk2Nm8&usp=drive_web

Donald Marshall Books 2 items

Donald Marshall F...   Donald Marshall S...

The compilation guide to Donald Marshall's information, presented as short documents. Read, print, download and share.

Donald Marshall Conspiratorium Room- Music Videos, Links, & News:
https://www.facebook.com/groups/Conspiratorium/

A place to learn; to privately post videos, links, and news related to the entertainment industry, cloning centers, Donald Marshall, and the Illuminati... Request to join.

Donald Marshall Public Figure Facebook Page:
https://www.facebook.com/donald.muktar.marshall

Donald Marshall's Public Figure page is run on his behalf, where posts from Donald Marshall's Facebook account are transferred to this page to allow all to post, comment, read and share Donald Marshall's information.

Rogue 1
https://www.facebook.com/Rogue1DM/

A Facebook group to learn more about vril parasites; microchip bodysnatching; human cloning; especially REM phase human cloning which **must** be known and stopped.

The Reference Palace:
https://www.facebook.com/TheReferencePalace

A Palace, where references [relating to the Illuminati's REM driven human cloning subculture and Donald Marshall's disclosures], are collected, catalogued, and collated for Donald Marshall.

whoisdonaldmarshall Instagram:
https://www.instagram.com/whoisdonaldmarshall/

Donald Marshall's Instagram account is run on his behalf, where posts from Donald Marshall's Facebook account are transferred to Instagram in order to reach a wider audience and allow many more to comment, read and share Donald Marshall's information.

All references in this document have been saved and backed-up; therefore if any link in this document, is ever deleted, modified etc. (online), let me know.

References

A Nightmare on Elm Street (1984) Film. Directed by Wes Craven. [DVD]. USA: New Line Cinema

Astral 7sight (2013a) *Illuminati Exposed 2013: Chemtrails, Atlantis, Clones, Drones & Vril Part 1/8*. [Online video]. June 23rd 2013. Available from: https://www.youtube.com/watch?v=UonnFuHLJKc&ab_channel=Astral7ight [Accessed 12th July 2015]

Astral 7sight (2013b) *Illuminati Exposed 2013: Chemtrails, Atlantis, Clones, Drones & Vril Part 2/8*. [Online video]. June 23rd 2013. Available from: https://www.youtube.com/watch?v=QPAXCwu5MIo&ab_channel=Astral7ight [Accessed 12th July 2015]

Astral 7sight (2013c) *Illuminati Exposed 2013: Chemtrails, Atlantis, Clones, Drones & Vril Part 3/8*. [Online video]. June 23rd 2013. Available from: https://www.youtube.com/watch?v=5zlJ0VQP444&ab_channel=Astral7ight [Accessed 12th July 2015]

Astral 7sight (2013d) *Illuminati Exposed 2013: Chemtrails, Atlantis, Clones, Drones & Vril Part 4/8*. [Online video]. June 23rd 2013. Available from: https://www.youtube.com/watch?v=dCGhrDEl-q8&ab_channel=Astral7ight [Accessed 12th July 2015]

Astral 7sight (2013e) *Illuminati Exposed 2013: Chemtrails, Atlantis, Clones, Drones & Vril Part 5/8*. [Online video]. June 23rd 2013. Available from: https://www.youtube.com/watch?v=EDyerA-k8Ic&ab_channel=Astral7ight [Accessed 12th July 2015]

Astral 7sight (2013f) *Illuminati Exposed 2013: Chemtrails, Atlantis, Clones, Drones & Vril Part 6/8*. [Online video]. June 23rd 2013. Available from: https://www.youtube.com/watch?v=iqQZPpXl2yg&ab_channel=Astral7ight [Accessed 12th July 2015]

Astral 7sight (2013g) *Illuminati Exposed 2013: Chemtrails, Atlantis, Clones, Drones & Vril Part 7/8*. [Online video]. June 23rd 2013. Available from: https://www.youtube.com/watch?v=WYZSOnyWwP8&ab_channel=Astral7ight [Accessed 12th July 2015]

Astral 7sight (2013h) *Illuminati Exposed 2013: Chemtrails, Atlantis, Clones, Drones & Vril Part 8/8*. [Online video]. June 23rd 2013. Available from: https://www.youtube.com/watch?v=Y18m0gPLQhM&ab_channel=Astral7ight [Accessed 12th July 2015]

Astral 7sight (2014) *Donald Marshall @ The Library (2012)* [Online video]. March 11th 2014. Available from: https://www.youtube.com/watch?v=-RfbXxzOzjY [Accessed 18th February 2016]

Avatar (2009) Film. Directed by James Cameron. [DVD]. UK: 20th Century Fox

AZLyrics (2011a) *DAVID GUETTA Lyrics "Titanium" (feat. Sia)* [Online] Available from: http://www.azlyrics.com/lyrics/davidguetta/titanium.html [Accessed February 19th 2016]

AZLyrics (2011b) *FLO RIDA Lyrics "Good Feeling"* [Online] Available from: http://www.azlyrics.com/lyrics/florida/goodfeeling.html [Accessed February 19th 2016]

AZLyrics (2012) *K'NAAN Lyrics "Is Anybody Out There?" (feat. Nelly Furtado).* [Online] Available from: http://www.azlyrics.com/lyrics/knaan/isanybodyoutthere.html [Accessed February 19th 2016]

Bryan Adams (2008) *Bryan Adams – Cuts Like A Knife* [Online video] October 30th 2008. Available from: https://www.youtube.com/watch?v=6VZhSkREYBc [February 19th 2016]

Daily Mail Online (2010) *The Queen's Loyal Serpent:400 years on, a painted over snake reappears on portrait of Elizabeth I* [Online] Available from: http://www.dailymail.co.uk/news/article-1255466/Mysterious-image-snake-appears-400-year-old-painting-Queen-Elizabeth-I.html [Accessed 16th February 2016]

David Guetta (2011) *David Guetta – Titanium ft. Sia (Official Video)* [Online video] December 20th 2011. Available from: https://www.youtube.com/watch?v=JRfuAukYTKg [February 19th 2016]

Donald Marshall Proboards (2012) *DONALD'S ORIGINAL LETTER TO THE PUBLIC..* [Online] Available from: http://donaldmarshall.proboards.com/thread/75/donalds-original-letter-public [Accessed: 28th July 2015]

Ehrsson, H.H., (2013) *Inspirational Lecture –Professor Henrik Ehrsson* [Online video] October 3rd 2013. Available from: https://www.youtube.com/watch?v=iR7HissYN2U&ab_channel=karolinskainstitutet [Accessed 2nd July 2015]

Eric Hastey (2012a) *Donald Marshall* [Online video]. May 14th 2012. Available from: https://www.youtube.com/watch?v=-AoNUkMXqKo [Accessed: 18th February 2016]

Eric Hastey (2012b) *Donald Marshall Clone Illuminati Interview Raw Interview Part 1-2* [Online video]. May 12th 2012. Available from: https://www.youtube.com/watch?v=IWqEvwAfWbI [Accessed: 18th February 2016]

Eric Hastey (2012c) *Donald Marshall Clone Illuminati Interview Raw Interview Part 2-2* [Online video]. May 12th 2012. Available from: https://www.youtube.com/watch?v=mymZCh_v01Q [Accessed: 18th February 2016]

Filipe Augusto (2007) *I'm Lovin' It* [Online video] January 28th 2007. Available from: https://www.youtube.com/watch?v=dI-xHMM8wXE [February 18th 2016]

Flo Rida (2011) *Flo Rida – Good Feeling [Official Video]* [Online video]. Oct 21st 2011. Available from: https://www.youtube.com/watch?v=3OnnDqH6Wj8 [Accessed: 18th February 2016]

H.J. Simpson (2015) *The Simpsons Two Party System | Tree House of Horror* [Online video]. October 17th 2015. Available from: https://www.youtube.com/watch?v=4v7XXSt9XRM [Accessed 18th February 2016]

Inception (2010) Film. Directed by Christopher Nolan. [DVD]. UK: Warner Bros. Pictures

Jeanice Barcelo (2013) *BNE Radio Show w/ guest Donald Marshall* [Online video]. March 9th 2013. Available from: https://www.youtube.com/watch?v=3uzgu4ekT3c&ab_channel=JeaniceBarcelo [Accessed 11th July 2015]

justintimberlakeVEVO (2009) *Justin Timberlake –I'm Lovin' It* [Online video] October 2nd 2009. Available from: https://www.youtube.com/watch?v=-IHcp8Pl_X4 [February 18th 2016]

KnaanVEVO (2012) *Is Anybody Out There? ft. Nelly Furtado* [Online video] March 1st 2008. Available from: https://www.youtube.com/watch?v=nevOsRGqL2c [February 19th 2016]

LyricsFreak (2016) *PRINCE Lyrics "Raspberry Beret"* [Online] Available from: http://www.lyricsfreak.com/p/prince/raspberry+beret_20111286.html [Accessed February 19th 2016]

Maroon5VEVO (2010) *Maroon 5 -Misery* [Online video] June 30th 2010. Available from: https://www.youtube.com/watch?v=6g6g2mvItp4 [February 19th 2016]

Marshall, D., (2015a) *Empowerment by Virtue of Golden Truth. Human Cloning: Specifically REM Driven Human Cloning. Summary Disclosure.* Unpublished.

Marshall, D., (2015b) *Empowerment by Virtue of Golden Truth. Human Cloning: Specifically REM Driven Human Cloning. Full Disclosure.* Unpublished.

Medical News Today (2015a) *ADD/ADHD: Causes, Symptoms and Research* [Online] Available from: http://www.medicalnewstoday.com/info/adhd/ [Accessed 18th February 2016]

Medical News Today (2015b) *What is Asperger's Syndrome?* [Online] Available from: http://www.medicalnewstoday.com/articles/7601.php [Accessed 18th February 2016]

Medline Plus (2016) *Riley-Day syndrome* [Online] Available from: https://www.nlm.nih.gov/medlineplus/ency/article/001387.htm [Accessed 18th February 2016]

Megadeth (2001) *The World Needs a Hero* [CD] USA: Sanctuary Records Group Ltd

MetroLyrics (2009) *PITBULL Lyrics "Shut It Down" (feat. Akon)* [Online] Available from: http://www.metrolyrics.com/shut-it-down-lyrics-pitbull.html [Accessed February 19th 2016]

♦MOONSTORMSATA♦ (2012) *Madness in the Fast Lane –Swedish Sisters (full)* [Online video]. June 20th 2012. Available from: https://www.youtube.com/watch?v=9-bIWm08eJc [Accessed: February 19th 2016]

NellyFurtadoVEVO (2009) *Nelly Furtado –Say It Right* [Online video] June 16th 2009. Available from: https://www.youtube.com/watch?v=6JnGBs88sL0 [February 18th 2016]

Nguyen, L., (2010) *Queen reminds Canadians reasons to be proud* [Online] Available from: http://www.canada.com/news/Queen+reminds+Canadians+reasons+proud/3239016/story.html [Accessed 18th February 2016]

Open Minds (2011) *Phil Schneider's incredible ET claims.* [Online] Available from: http://www.openminds.tv/phil-schneiders-incredible-et-claims/9982 [Accessed 9th May 2015]

Peterjochu (2012) *Prince – Raspberry Beret* [Online video] April 1st 2012. Available from: http://www.metacafe.com/watch/8305118/prince_raspberry_beret/ [February 18th 2016]

Petkova, V. I., and Ehrsson, H.H., (2008) *If I Were You: Perceptual Illusion of Body Swapping,* PLoS ONE, Volume 3, Issue 12, pp. 1-9

PitbullVEVO (2009) *Pitbull –Shut It Down ft. Akon* [Online video] November 29th 2009. Available from: https://www.youtube.com/watch?v=QECUFmEPbU0 [February 18th 2016]

Robin Francis (2008) *Lady –Kenny Rogers* [Online video] January 11th 2008. Available from: https://www.youtube.com/watch?v=ZYRfUoR9Q4Y [February 18th 2016]

Roadrunner Records (2012) *Nickelback – This Means War [OFFICIAL VIDEO]* [Online video] March 29th 2012. Available from: https://www.youtube.com/watch?v=exlGc8eFXI0 [February 19th 2016]

Schneider, P., (1995) *Phil Schneider Documentary of truth about Aliens & UFO's & our Government.* [Online video]. September 21st 2013. Available from: https://www.youtube.com/watch?v=Oljrjxnixtw&ab_channel=AliensAmongUs [Accessed: 10th May 2015]

Schneider, P., (1996) *Phil Schneider's Last Speech ~ Two Months Before His Assassination ~ Aliens & Underground Bases* [Online video]. November 24th 2013. Available from: https://www.youtube.com/watch?v=Slgb5U-OqFM&ab_channel=FallofMedia [Accessed: 10th May 2015]

Science Channel (2014) *How to Grow a New Fingertip | World's Strangest.* [Online video] June 16th 2014. Available from: https://www.youtube.com/watch?v=DtBUM51t4iw&ab [Accessed 23rd June 2015]

Sleepdex (2016) *Stages of Sleep* [Online] Available from: http://www.sleepdex.org/stages.htm [Accessed: 16th February 2016]

The Independent (2012) *Michael Fagan: 'Her nightie was one of those liberty prints, down to her knees'* [Online] Available from: http://www.independent.co.uk/news/people/profiles/michael-fagan-her-nightie-was-one-of-those-liberty-prints-down-to-her-knees-7179547.html [Accessed 18th February 2016]

The Live Room powered by Warner Music (2012) *Flo Rida - Whistle (Official Video)* [Online video] May 24th 2012. Available from: https://www.youtube.com/watch?v=cSnkWzZ7ZAA [February 18th 2016]

The Naked Scientists (2009) *A rush of blood to the head* [Online] Available from: http://www.thenakedscientists.com/HTML/science-news/news/1754/ [Accessed 16th February 2016]

The Prodigy (2008a) *The Prodigy –Breathe (Official Video)* [Online video] May 27th 2008. Available from: https://www.youtube.com/watch?v=6_PAHbqq-o4 [February 18th 2016]

The Prodigy (2008b) *The Prodigy –Firestarter (Official Video)* [Online video] May 27th 2008. Available from: https://www.youtube.com/watch?v=wmin5WkOuPw [February 18th 2016]

TrainVEVO (2012) *Train –Drive By* [Online video] February 15th 2012. Available from: https://www.youtube.com/watch?v=oxqnFJ3lp5k [February 18th 2016]

Vincent Eastwood (2013) *Illuminati Cloning Programs, Sex and Murder Cults and Reptilians! 26Feb2013* [Online video] February 26th 2013. Available from: https://www.youtube.com/watch?v=M_1UiFeV5Jg&ab_channel=VincentEastwood [10th July 2015]

Walcutt, D. L., (2013) *Stages of Sleep.* [Online] Available from: http://psychcentral.com/lib/stages-of-sleep/ [Accessed 16th February 2016]

Legislation

Computer Misuse Act (1990) Section 3A, *Making, supplying or obtaining articles for use in offence under section 1 or 3* [Online] Available from: http://www.legislation.gov.uk/ukpga/1990/18/section/3A [Accessed 8th May 2015]

Enterprise and Regulatory Reform Act (2013) Section 17, *Disclosures not protected unless believed to be made in the public interest.* [Online] Available from: http://www.legislation.gov.uk/ukpga/2013/24/section/17/enacted [Accessed 8th May 2015]

Public Interest Disclosure Act (1998) Section 43B, *Disclosures qualifying for protection.* [Online] Available from: http://www.legislation.gov.uk/ukpga/1998/23/section/1 [Accessed 8th May 2015]

Serious Crime Act (2015) Section 41 3ZA, *Unauthorised acts causing, or creating risk of, serious damage.* [Online] Available from: http://www.legislation.gov.uk/ukpga/2015/9/section/41/enacted [Accessed 8th May 2015]

Made in the USA
Las Vegas, NV
19 January 2025